SILENT IN AN EVIL TIME

Garfield County Libraries
New Castle Branch
402 West Main Street
New Castle, Colorado 81647
(970) 984-2346
www.garfieldlibraries.org

JACK BATTEN

SILENT IN AN EVIL TIME

The Brave War of Edith Cavell

TUNDRA BOOKS

As a nurse, Edith often cared for children. She looked after this young boy in
1903 at the Shoreditch Infirmary for London's poorest patients. (The Royal London
Hospital Archives)

DISCARDED FROM
GARFIELD COUNTY PUBLIC
LIBRARY SYSTEM

Copyright © 2007 by Jack Batten

Published in Canada by Tundra Books,
75 Sherbourne Street, Toronto, Ontario M5A 2P9

Published in the United States by Tundra Books of Northern New York,
P.O. Box 1030, Plattsburgh, New York 12901

Library of Congress Control Number: 2006940129

All rights reserved. The use of any part of this publication reproduced, transmitted in any
form or by any means, electronic, mechanical, photocopying, recording, or otherwise, or stored
in a retrieval system, without the prior written consent of the publisher – or, in case of
photocopying or other reprographic copying, a licence from the Canadian Copyright Licensing
Agency – is an infringement of the copyright law.

Library and Archives Canada Cataloguing in Publication

Batten, Jack, 1932-
Silent in an evil time : the brave war of Edith Cavell / Jack Batten.

Includes bibliographical references and index.
ISBN 978-0-88776-737-1

1. Cavell, Edith, 1865-1915 – Juvenile literature.
2. Nurses – Great Britain – Biography – Juvenile literature.
3. World War, 1914-1918 – Belgium – Juvenile literature.
I. Title.

D630.C3B38 2007   j940.4'76092   C2006-906825-9

We acknowledge the financial support of the Government of Canada through the Book
Publishing Industry Development Program (BPIDP) and that of the Government of Ontario
through the Ontario Media Development Corporation's Ontario Book Initiative.
We further acknowledge the support of the Canada Council for the Arts and the Ontario Arts
Council for our publishing program.

ONTARIO ARTS COUNCIL
CONSEIL DES ARTS DE L'ONTARIO

The author gratefully acknowledges the financial support of the Canada Council for the Arts.

Design: Scott Richardson

Printed and bound in Canada

1 2 3 4 5 6   12 11 10 09 08 07

FOR MADDY

—

CONTENTS

Chapter One

EDITH'S NARROW ESCAPE

Edith Cavell heard the crash of soldiers' boots at the front door below. The sound could mean only one thing – the Germans had come to the clinic! Looking after a ward of patients on the second floor, Edith knew that she had no more than five minutes to get Arthur Wood out of sight. If the Germans caught an English soldier among the clinic's patients, Edith would lose her freedom and possibly her life.

It was a February morning in 1915, six months after the Germans occupied Belgium in the invasion that began the First World War. Edith, an English nurse, lived and worked in Belgium's capital city of Brussels, where she ran the country's only training clinic for nurses. Unknown to the German occupiers, Edith was using the clinic to smuggle British soldiers back to England.

These young graduates from Edith's clinic became the first fully trained nurses to provide services in Belgium's hospitals, schools, and private nursing homes. (The Royal London Hospital Archives)

Hundreds of the soldiers were caught behind enemy lines during the German advance through Belgium, and Edith joined a secret organization dedicated to hiding the soldiers and guiding them north to the Dutch border, on a route that took them home. On the February day when the Germans made their surprise visit to the clinic, one of the escaping Englishmen was with Edith in the second-floor ward. The soldier was an army private named Arthur Wood.

—

Edith thought of Wood as a special case among the dozens of soldiers she had already helped to escape. He was barely twenty, and looked even younger. With his smooth innocent face, Wood could be mistaken for a boy in his middle teens. An energetic young man, impatient after several days concealed in the clinic, he was keen to be on his way to Holland. Edith put Wood to work as an orderly to keep him occupied during his restless wait. He handled simple duties, assisting the nurses as they tended to the sick and injured Belgian citizens. And he was doing precisely that when the sound of German soldiers echoed from down below.

Arthur froze.

"Be quick, Arthur, and do what I tell you," Edith said. "And please stay calm." Edith, herself, was always calm. She was also a fast thinker.

She told Wood to remove his clothes down to his underwear and to put on a hospital gown. As he followed Edith's instructions, she turned back the covers on an empty bed and motioned him to climb underneath them.

The crack of German boots became louder. Edith knew that the soldiers had started up the stairs from the first floor.

"Stay in the bed, Arthur," she said. "You are going to be a patient. Please see if you can act like a person who is sick. But whatever you do, Arthur, don't open your mouth."

In appearance, Wood could pass for an ordinary Belgian kid, but he could never talk like one. He spoke little French, which was one of Belgium's national languages, and he certainly knew no German.

The sounds of the German soldiers told Edith that they had reached the top of the stairs. She placed a screen around Wood's bed. Then she turned to the door, just as a German officer and his soldiers entered the ward.

Edith was sure that German officials hadn't caught on to the secret activities that were happening in the clinic. She and the others in her organization were careful to keep the English soldiers out of sight. The Germans must be making this unannounced call to show Edith that they were in charge in Brussels. German soldiers were running the city, and they could barge in anywhere they wanted.

"Yes?" Edith said to the officer in French. "How can I help you?"

The officer was brisk and demanding. He let Edith know who was giving the orders. He said he intended to inspect the ward. In fact, he was going to take a tour of the entire clinic. Edith informed him that all of the patients were Belgians. The officer walked around the ward, looking at the men in the beds, asking them questions about their health. The patients answered in few words. As the officer checked the men, he seemed to accept that nothing was out of the ordinary.

Then he came to the bed with the screen around it.

"The boy in this bed is far too ill to be disturbed," Edith said. She was polite, but firm. "He cannot possibly answer questions."

The German officer said he would make his own judgment about that. He pulled back the screen and peered in. Arthur Wood was playing his role. His heart may have been pounding, but he lay under the covers, eyes closed, his face still. He looked younger than ever, and he was giving his best imitation of a very sick boy. The officer hesitated, taking all the time he needed to satisfy himself that the young man in the bed was who he was supposed to be – a Belgian patient in a ward at Edith Cavell's clinic.

A minute or two ticked by while the officer examined Wood from the bedside. Edith was tense. She had no idea what the officer could be looking for. All she knew was that he was making her anxious, though she showed no sign.

Finally, the officer appeared satisfied. He stepped away from Arthur's bedside and turned toward the door. Edith hurried to put the screen back in place while the officer led his soldiers out of the room and off to inspect the other wards.

While the Germans completed the rest of their rounds, Edith followed. She knew that the danger hadn't passed; other escaping British soldiers were hiding in the basement. But, to Edith's relief, the German officer checked only the top floors. His tour lasted almost an hour before he and his soldiers finally marched out of the clinic's front door.

In the ward on the second floor, Arthur Wood hopped from the bed behind the screen. His heart had stopped racing, and he wore a broad smile. Edith told him he had done a fine acting job, and he should feel proud of himself. Wood wanted to hug Edith, but she was as old as his mother, not someone he should wrap his arms around. He thanked her sincerely, and that was enough.

A few days later, a man in Edith's secret organization guided Wood to the border. He had no trouble crossing into Holland, and within a week, he was home in England, reporting to his army regiment.

—

Back in Brussels, the close call with Arthur Wood didn't stop Edith from carrying on her dangerous work. In the months that followed, hundreds of other British soldiers fleeing the Germans came through the clinic. Edith had more close calls, but she never hesitated to take whatever risks were needed to save each one of her soldiers.

Edith's brave work made her the greatest English heroine of the First World War. She paid a terrible price for her service to her country, but she remained forever in the hearts of young men like Arthur Wood, who owed their lives to her.

"I was hiding in the clinic of which your daughter was Matron," Wood wrote to Edith's mother in England. "She treated me like my own Mother would have done and proved herself to be the very best friend I ever had."

Chapter Two

EDITH FINDS NURSING

Edith's unexpected path to heroism began in the quiet and cozy English village of Swardeston, where she was born Edith Louisa Cavell on December 5, 1865. Swardeston lies five kilometers southwest of the city of Norwich, in the county of Norfolk on England's east coast. Norwich, the county's capital and its commercial center, is a handsome city most famous for its ancient and mighty cathedral.

Everybody in Swardeston recognized Edith's father as the village's leading citizen. He was the Reverend Frederick Cavell, vicar of St. Mary the Virgin Anglican Church from 1863 until his death in 1910. The Reverend Cavell was punctual, strict, and industrious. He never missed a church service or any other obligation. Before he married his wife, Louisa, in 1863, he sent her to a finishing school to learn the rules of etiquette and the other social skills that he thought a vicar's wife needed for success.

Edith was an athletic and confident teenager. She loved lawn tennis, ice-skating, and dancing at parties. (The Royal London Hospital Archives)

Edith was born in 1865 in this eighteenth-century redbrick farmhouse in the Norfolk village of Swardeston. (Jack Batten)

The Reverend Cavell was a man who paid close attention to every detail of his family's life.

Edith was the first Cavell child, followed by three more: Florence, born in 1867; Lillian, in 1870; and son, Jack, in 1873.

—

From the time she was a little girl, Edith was good-natured, athletic, and pretty. She loved to skate in the winter, and she was crazy about lawn tennis in the summer. She taught Sunday school at her father's church, and she developed a talent for painting in watercolor, a hobby that stayed with her for the rest of her life.

The Reverend Cavell took charge of Edith's education, enrolling her in

When Edith was a teenager, she drew these illustrations for greeting cards, which she sold to raise money to help pay off the debt on the vicarage that her father built in Swardeston. (The Royal London Hospital Archives)

Norwich's secondary school for only a short time and teaching her most of the lessons at home. (He also taught the other three children for different periods.) A demanding instructor, some of the subjects he gave Edith seemed beyond the reach of a young girl. When her father had her study the difficult writings of the German philosophers, Edith raised no objection. She liked hard work, and she liked to satisfy her father.

When Edith turned sixteen, the Reverend Cavell admitted that she needed more education than he could provide. He sent her to three different boarding schools in the next three years. The first two were far from home, one in London and the other in the west of England. Edith's father thought it was good for her to spend time away from her mother because,

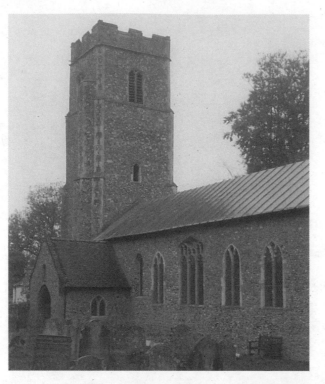

Edith's father, the Reverend Frederick Cavell, became vicar of St. Mary the Virgin Anglican Church in Swardeston in 1863 and remained in the position for the rest of his life. (Jack Batten)

St. Mary's was a small village church, but the Reverend Cavell filled the pews for his sermons each Sunday until his death in 1910, at the age of eighty-five. (Jack Batten)

in his opinion, his wife, Louisa, had grown too possessive of their oldest daughter. Despite Edith's absences from home – at the schools and during the long periods she later lived in distant parts of England and in Belgium – Louisa Cavell never lost the habit of depending on her more than on anyone else in the family.

The third of the three boarding schools had a lasting effect on Edith. It was called Laurel Court, in the town of Peterborough, in the county to the west of Norfolk. Among its subjects, Laurel Court taught French, a language that became crucial to Edith, and the school's piano lessons gave her another means of artistic expression besides her painting.

But it was Margaret Gibson, the school's principal and a woman of immense self-confidence, whose personal example opened Edith's eyes. A rare feminist, Miss Gibson offered living proof that a woman, granted half a chance, could match a man in accomplishment and authority. Miss Gibson naturally assumed that she was the equal of any male she encountered, and Edith was in awe.

—

By the summer of 1886, when she was twenty, Edith had blossomed into a mature and attractive young woman. She had a trim figure, striking blue-gray eyes, and dark brown hair, which she pulled back from her forehead in a dramatic sweep. She knew how to make conversation in any company, and at a party, she was first on the dance floor. During one Christmas festivity, she danced so often and so enthusiastically that her feet bled and ruined her brand-new shoes.

Of all the young men who were keen on Edith, one seemed to be the perfect match. He was Eddy Cavell, a second cousin, three years older than Edith – a pleasant-looking, redheaded man. Edith came to know Eddy well during the summers, when their families spent holidays together at a beach resort on the North Sea. The young couple often took long walks together. They caught shrimp from the sea. And Eddy read to

Edith from a book of Robert Browning's poetry as she painted. Everybody thought they made an ideal couple.

But one obstacle stood in the way. Eddy suffered from a "nervous disorder." The condition also affected his mother. Because of it, Eddy couldn't deal with such ordinary activities as riding on a train. He often felt anxious, and he lacked the confidence to go into law practice, like his father and grandfather had. Eddy settled for a simpler job as manager of a small farm. For fear that he would pass on the nervous disorder to any children he might have, Eddy came to the conclusion that he should never marry.

Edith was disappointed by Eddy's decision, but she didn't let it crush her. She eventually applied to nursing the love and dedication that she would have put into her marriage. Like Eddy, Edith never considered marrying anyone else in later years.

—

To make her way in the world, Edith decided to become a governess. She got her first position with the family of a vicar named Charles Powell, who lived in the village of Steeple Bumstead in Essex County, south of Norfolk. The Reverend Powell and his wife had four children from the ages of six to eleven. As governess, Edith looked after everything: what the children ate, how they played, their schooling, their clothing, their music lessons, and their discipline. She was strict, but fair. Edith had a knack for keeping the Powell children under firm control and filling them with fun at the same time. They adored her, and Edith returned their affection. Three years later, the Reverend Powell decided the children had outgrown the need for a governess. The time had come for their beloved Edith to leave Steeple Bumstead, and the four young Powells wept. As she bid them farewell, tears ran down Edith's cheeks.

Following her time with the Powell family, Edith went on a holiday to Europe, financed by a small inheritance from a relative. For her, the highlight of the trip came in the German province of Bavaria, where she visited the Free Hospital. The institution offered care at no charge to patients who couldn't afford medical treatment. Edith was so impressed by the hospital's generosity that she donated part of her inheritance to purchase new medical equipment. Around the Free Hospital, Edith earned a special name from the staff and patients. She was "the English Angel."

If the experience in Bavaria gave Edith the idea that she might choose nursing as her profession, four more positions as governess still lay ahead. Three were with families not far from Swardeston, but the fourth was different and exceptional. The principal at Laurel Court, the formidable Margaret Gibson, used her contacts to secure a job for Edith that took her out of England – to a city that would be central to her future. Edith went to work for the François family, whose home was in a grand house on the most beautiful avenue in Brussels.

—

Belgium wasn't far from England in distance – little more than sixty kilometers across the English Channel – but to a young woman like Edith, it was light-years away in history and culture. Her new employer, Paul François, was a leading lawyer in Brussels, and he, his wife, and their four young children lived in a large and gracious house on Avenue Louise. The street was the city's pride, several lanes wide, and lined for its entire length with four rows of chestnut trees. The François mansion blended naturally into these gorgeous surroundings, and as the governess of the house, Edith found herself among Brussels' most sophisticated society. Life back in simple Swardeston was nothing like life on stylish Avenue Louise.

Edith took full part in the François family's activities. She carried out her job as governess, winning the children's affections just as she had at the Powell house, but the François parents also included her at parties and on holidays in glamorous resorts. At first, Edith wasn't entirely comfortable during the three-hour Sunday lunches and the even longer dinners, with the ongoing gossip and chatter. But she grew to enjoy the occasions, easily holding up her end of conversations.

Edith developed such confidence that she gave Paul François a piece of her mind at one luncheon. When François made a rude remark about England's Queen Victoria, Edith stood up from her chair and told Monsieur François she wasn't going to sit there while someone, even her employer, insulted the monarch of her country. Then she strode out of the room. Edith thought any patriotic English person would have reacted in the same bold way. François had to admit that he admired the governess' spirit.

—

During the years Edith worked for the François family, she took annual summer holidays at home in Swardeston. For two or three weeks at a time, she sank back into the life that had been familiar to her since childhood – the life of tennis, church, watercolors, and long walks through the countryside. Nineteenth-century English people habitually walked great distances, and Edith was a spectacular example of the female of the species. It was nothing for her to take brisk hikes of several hours on the roads and paths around Swardeston. She had lots of time to read, which she did widely, and Charles Dickens was her favorite novelist. Among poets, she admired William Wordsworth, the writer who looked on poetry as a higher calling.

Both of Edith's sisters, Florence and Lillian, had chosen nursing as their profession, and they were launched on rewarding careers. Jack, the youngest Cavell child, lived in the shadow of his accomplished sisters. He found a job in the offices of the Norwich Union Insurance Society in the nearby city, staying with the company for his entire working life, not rising far up the ranks. Jack was bitter and took out his disappointments in long nights of drinking in bars. He never married, though he had a romance with a barmaid. The Cavell family considered the relationship unworthy for the son of a vicar, and the Reverend Cavell left it to Edith to break up her brother's romance. Edith handled the difficult job with tact, but Jack never forgave her, not even in later years when Edith became England's great heroine.

—

In the spring of 1895, when Edith was twenty-nine, the Reverend Cavell became ill, probably with pneumonia. Mrs. Cavell begged Edith to come home and look after her father. Edith wasted no time in returning to the Swardeston vicarage, but she was sad to leave her job with the François family, and sad to move from Brussels, which she thought of as her second home. Her family, however, had first claim on her loyalties.

Edith cared for her father through the summer, providing him with the nursing he so desperately needed. It might have been expected that Mrs. Cavell would have asked Florence or Lillian to look after their father, since they were trained nurses. But she turned to Edith, the daughter she most relied on. Edith performed so capably that the Reverend Cavell returned to his church full-time by early autumn.

The experience with her father came as a final revelation for Edith. Over the years, since her visit to the Free Hospital in Bavaria, she had been thinking about nursing as a career. At last, feeling the satisfaction of bringing the Reverend Cavell back to health, she made up her mind once and for all: She would train to become a full-time nurse.

Chapter Three

THE WOMAN WHO INVENTED NURSING

F ar more than anyone else, Florence Nightingale shaped the profession that Edith was about to enter. Before Nightingale, nursing – as we know it in the modern world – didn't exist. In the mid-nineteenth century, nurses were of two kinds, both incapable of giving proper care. One kind was made up of members of Anglican and Catholic religious orders, and while good-hearted, the women were often more interested in saving the souls of their patients than in treating their illnesses. The second kind came from the lowest classes. They were women who carried out little more than house-maid's chores, who sometimes got drunk on the job. Neither sort of nurse had formal training in looking after sick people, nor were they expected to do much beyond keeping the patients as comfortable as possible while they waited to die. Then along came Florence Nightingale.

—

Sixteen-year-old Florence Nightingale (seated) and her sister, Parthenope, lived the pampered life of the very rich in nineteenth-century England. (The Toronto Reference Library)

Florence was as different from Edith as day is from night. She was born in 1820 to a life of privilege. Her immediate family – father, mother, and older sister, Parthenope – divided their time between two handsome country estates. When the family traveled to London for parties and balls, they stayed in lavish hotel suites. From her childhood to her death in 1910, Florence Nightingale moved in circles that included England's powerful elite.

Florence's father was quick to recognize that his younger daughter had a brilliant mind. He made sure she received a broader education than most boys of the time. Florence, who was Anglican, believed that God appeared to her on February 7, 1837, when she was seventeen, and called her to His service. Florence decided that the service lay in nursing. Driven to care for the ill, she was forever rushing to the bedsides of sick friends and relatives, and she developed an instinct for treating people in medical need. With her intellectual nature, Florence researched every corner of the health profession. She visited hospitals in England and on the continent, learning the techniques of nursing and keeping notes on each hospital's methods.

Florence's parents opposed their daughter's fascination with medicine every step of the way. To them and to everyone else of their class, nursing was no activity for a lady. They expected her to marry someone of her own social standing and raise a family. Like Edith Cavell, Florence Nightingale remained single; unlike Edith, Florence had the money to follow her passion for healing wherever she wanted it to take her.

—

Florence's chance to put the ideas she formed about nursing into effect arrived when Britain entered the Crimean War in the spring of 1854. The war pitted Britain, France, and Turkey against Russia, all the countries quarreling over small differences. On the battlefields, the fighting took place in a part of the world that few English people could have found on a map. It was in the Crimea, a remote region of southwest Russia on the Black Sea. Britain sent fifty thousand poorly equipped troops to the distant battleground, led by incompetent generals. From the beginning, the soldiers suffered from disease, wounds, and medical neglect.

In response, Florence Nightingale recruited thirty-eight nurses, and under her leadership, the nursing team sailed to the war zone to save lives. They landed in Turkey, in November 1854, to a cold reception from the British officers and the army doctors. Both groups looked on Florence as a pushy woman, sticking her nose into a place where she wasn't wanted.

Florence ignored the opposition. She took over a hospital in an abandoned Turkish army barracks in Scutari, a suburb of Turkey's major city of Constantinople. The building had no running water, few beds, and was unready in every imaginable way to receive sick and wounded soldiers. Florence soon put things in order. She and her team scrubbed away the building's filth, she spent her own money on beds and equipment, and she inspired her nurses to work with discipline and efficiency.

—

Over the next many months, thousands of soldiers who needed medical treatment were transported by ship across the Black Sea, from the Crimean battlefields to Scutari. At the hospital, Florence created an institution so different from other military hospitals that it amounted to a revolution in caregiving. She emphasized fresh air, pure water, and washed sheets on every bed. She preached good hygiene and plenty of nourishing food.

Today, we take for granted that hospitals, even at scenes of war, meet a minimum standard of cleanliness. But in the 1850s, such a notion was unheard of. Medical science hadn't yet grasped the concept of germs, which spread disease. But Florence's ideas about hygienic conditions made an enormous difference in the speed of healing among the soldiers and on the rate of their deaths. Even the military doctors, who were so

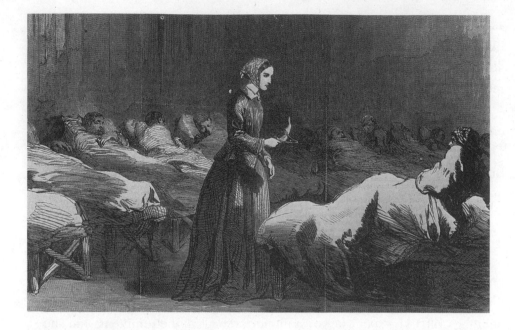

Florence Nightingale ran a military hospital for almost two years in the Crimean War of the mid-1850s. Her rounds of the wards each night made her famous as the "Lady with the Lamp," though the lamp she carried bore no resemblance to the one in this picture from The Illustrated London News *of Feb. 24, 1855. Florence's real lamp was described as "a candle inside an accordion-style shade that could be folded flat," which she held over her head.* (The Library of Congress, Washington, D.C.)

scornful of Florence, had to admit that far fewer men died at Scutari than expected, and those who survived improved more quickly than the doctors thought possible.

Florence, working eighteen hours a day, performed more nursing than any of her staff. She didn't turn away from the soldiers with the most festering wounds, or the worst cases of dysentery. At night, she wrote long reports to the government in London, explaining her methods and making her case for money and equipment. Before finally resting her head on the pillow each night, she took one last tour of the hospital wards. She walked the four kilometers of beds, lighting her way with a small Turkish lamp held over her head. The men idolized Florence as the "Lady with the Lamp."

———

At home in England, the Lady with the Lamp turned into a famous figure. The war made the front pages of every newspaper, and Florence Nightingale's nursing became an exciting part of the story. In the spring of 1856, a peace treaty brought an end to the war, which had produced few results apart from killing and maiming thousands of men on both sides.

The following autumn, Florence traveled back to England. She had spent twenty-two months in Turkey, taken three trips from Scutari to the battlefields, and survived an illness that almost cost her life. In England, she was revered and celebrated, though Florence proved to be an elusive subject for her admirers; what she didn't want for herself was celebrity. But it was beyond doubt that Florence's achievements at Scutari had raised the status of nursing as a profession. It was now respectable, as it had never been before, for a decent Englishwoman to become a nurse. Nursing itself was now looked on as something that could save lives, not just comfort those who were dying.

———

Florence Nightingale was an eccentric person. Just how odd she was became clear in the decades after her return from the war. In that long period, she lived much of her life as a recluse, in a house that her father bought for her in London's posh Mayfair district. From her late thirties to her death at age ninety, Florence rarely left her home. Instead, she devoted every waking hour to reading and writing about hospitals and the people who worked in them. Nobody knew more about the subject than she did. At the request of the British government, she wrote an eight-hundred-page report called "Notes Affecting the Health, Efficiency and Hospital

Administration of the British Army." The document was her first shot in the long and successful campaign to introduce her ideas about clean water, warm clothing, and trained nurses to both military and civilian hospitals.

She wrote about the training of nurses in *Notes on Nursing*, a book that was accepted as the last word on the matter and that remained in print for decades. The book changed the nature of nursing forever. Nurses in England would no longer be excessively religious or hopelessly alcoholic. Instead, they would be women who received training in the lessons of effective patient care. They would be taught to understand the instructions of doctors and surgeons. They would be dedicated professionals.

This was the kind of nurse who graduated from the school established at St. Thomas' Hospital in London in the late 1850s. The school, which was named the Nightingale Training Hospital for Nurses, adopted Florence's lessons, and the nurses who graduated from it, and from all the other hospital teaching institutions just like it, became the nursing profession's models. Through her ideas and influence, Florence Nightingale became the founder of modern nursing.

—

Edith Cavell never met Florence Nightingale, and it's unlikely that they ever corresponded, though Nightingale was a prodigious letter-writer. When Edith set off on a career in nursing in 1896, Florence was seventy-six years old and past the period of her greatest activity. Still, Edith was as aware as any other young Englishwoman of Florence's influential work. She would soon study *Notes on Nursing* as part of her training. She would come to understand the Nightingale principles because they were the basis of the profession that Edith had come to choose for her own.

OPPOSITE: *After her return from the Crimean War, Florence wrote countless reports and books about health care and the training of nurses. Her influence changed the profession of nursing forever.* (The Library of Congress, Washington, D.C.)

Chapter Four

NURSE EDITH

On September 3, 1896, at the age of thirty, Edith entered the London Hospital (known simply as the London) to begin four years of training. The London occupied many buildings on acres of land on Whitechapel Road, a wide and chaotic street that ran through the slums of the city's East End. Traditionally, the East End was the first home for poor immigrants to England, and in Edith's time, the area took in the country's largest population of Jewish refugees from eastern Europe. Edith could have done her training at a hospital in a more prosperous neighborhood. But she chose to work and live at the London, where she knew she would be nursing the poorest patients.

The London opened its doors in 1740. One of its early surgeons, Sir William Blizard, gave the hospital its motto: THE PATIENT COMES FIRST. As the words suggest, the London grew famous for the unselfishness of its

From her childhood to her adult years, Edith loved to sketch and to paint in watercolor. She drew this unidentified London scene in 1902, when she was night superintendent at London's St. Pancras Infirmary. (The Royal London Hospital Archives)

surgeons, including Sir William, who must have had astonishingly hardy health since he didn't retire until he passed his ninetieth birthday. But Sir William's durability made him an exception among early surgeons; as a group, they tended to die young. In the days of primitive instruments and of diagnoses that were far from scientific, surgeons put in weary days of performing operations with a high rate of failure. Though surgical techniques greatly improved in the late nineteenth century, surgeons' lives were, more often than not, short and hard. The pattern seemed to have been set by John Harrison, the London's very first surgeon, who took up his practice at age twenty-two and died just thirteen years later. The official cause of death was overwork.

The demands on the nurses at the London were just as unforgiving. When Edith started out as a probationary nurse, one of the staff of six hundred nurses, her day opened with the ringing of a bell at 6:00 in the morning, and it didn't end until 9:20 at night, when she went off duty and ate her supper. She was never idle during all those hours. She learned the skills of nursing by working alongside senior nurses, who were in charge of wards of patients, fifty-six beds to each ward. Edith attended lectures, absorbing the principles that had been developed by Florence Nightingale. As a probationer, she had the responsibility of cleaning and dusting the wards. Since each ward was heated by a large fireplace, clearing the soot was an endless task.

In theory, Edith was allowed time for meals during the day, but in a busy hospital, the reality was that nurses were lucky if they could leave their patients long enough for tea and a bun. Porridge turned up at every meal: porridge at breakfast, porridge and mincemeat at dinner, porridge and cold beef on Sundays. The one treat at the evening meal was a choice of beer or stout, and Edith didn't say no to the occasional beer.

She had one day off every two weeks, and used the free day for doing her laundry, writing letters, and taking walks. Social life was almost non-existent, and nurses were absolutely forbidden from associating with

Nurses at the London Hospital worked hard to keep the wards clean, bright, and cheery. Above is Sophia Ward, named after an eighteenth-century English princess. (The Royal London Hospital Archives)

doctors and other men in the hospital, except in the line of duty. If a nurse so much as sighed in the presence of a handsome surgeon, it was reason for dismissal.

—

Partway into her second year as a probationer, Edith was assigned to three months' emergency service in the town of Maidstone, southeast of London. A terrible epidemic of typhoid fever broke out in the town during the autumn of 1897. Edith was later remembered as the nurse who brought toys to Maidstone's children.

The location of the London Hospital, shown here in the 1890s shortly before Edith arrived to take her training, placed it among the city's poorest citizens in the East End. (The Royal London Hospital Archives)

For her third year, Edith was placed on the London's private nursing staff and attended patients in their homes. Back at the London full-time for her fourth and final year, Edith was appointed staff nurse in the hospital's Mellish Ward, where she had the bad luck to work under a bullying senior nurse named Lillian Gough. Edith wasn't happy to be singled out for Gough's harsh criticism, but she turned the senior nurse's treatment into one of the wry jokes she was noted for. She gave Mellish Ward a nickname: Hellish.

—

But the person at the London who struck fear into the heart of every nurse was Eva Luckes. From 1880 to 1919, Luckes was employed as the

The imposing woman in black is Eva Luckes, the often-feared Matron at the London Hospital. The class shown here is from 1892, four years before Edith arrived at the hospital to begin her nurse's training. (The Royal London Hospital Archives)

hospital's Matron, the official with the responsibility of training and grading each nurse. Luckes knew her business. She gave lectures on nursing techniques. She had powerful influence with the doctors and administrators at the hospital. And she kept the probationary nurses under such close observation that she felt confident in writing long reports on every woman who passed through the hospital's system.

Luckes looked and behaved like a younger Queen Victoria. She was plump and bossy. She had strong opinions, particularly about her nurses, and would never listen to a view different from her own. She was often harsh in her judgments, and though it was the last thing Luckes would admit, she could be mistaken in her written assessments.

Luckes' final report on Edith, at the end of her four years of training, put Edith in a poor light. "Cavell was not a success as a Staff Nurse," Luckes wrote. "She was not methodical nor observant and she over-estimated her own powers. Her intentions were excellent, and she was conscientious without being quite reliable as a Nurse." Few of the women at the London came in for generous words from their Matron, but in Edith's case, Luckes got her report spectacularly wrong. Everything about Edith's later career showed her to possess all the qualities that Luckes was unable to detect. If Edith weren't methodical, observant, and reliable, she would never have succeeded as Matron of the Brussels clinic.

It may have been that Luckes used her blunt reports on the nurses to spur those she criticized so sharply to higher accomplishments. But it's beyond question that Edith admired Luckes as an administrator and used her as the model when Edith later became the Matron in Brussels. Edith seems to have had respect, and even affection, for Luckes. Over the years, she stayed in touch with her by mail, keeping Luckes up to date on her life after the London. Edith's correspondence had a friendly and confiding tone. One letter in July 1901 reported an incident of a man robbing Edith of her money in a London street. Other letters asked Luckes for help in finding better nursing posts. Luckes always responded, and it was she who arranged Edith's first nursing position in January 1901.

—

The job was as night superintendent at the St. Pancras Infirmary in the middle of London, and it called for enormous stamina. Apart from the physical demands that went with working through the night and trying to sleep in the daytime, Edith treated the most impoverished and desperate patients. St. Pancras was a Poor Law Institution, dedicated to serving the penniless people of the community. As ever, Edith was attentive and sympathetic to those in her care.

When she won a better paying job two years later, it was once again in a Poor Law Institution in London, this time at the Shoreditch Infirmary, where she was made Assistant Matron. Among her patients at Shoreditch,

Edith became a favorite of the costermongers – traders who sold all sorts of goods from carts, which they pulled through London's streets. Costermongers wore clothes embroidered with pearl buttons, and they entertained their customers with jokes and funny patter. Despite the colorful costumes and outgoing personalities, costermongers lived difficult lives, working long days exposed to every illness. When they entered Shoreditch for medical treatment, they asked for Edith, the Assistant Matron who treated them with humor and compassion.

—

After four years at Shoreditch, Edith resigned to take a four-month trip through Europe with a nurse named Eveline Dickinson. It was the longest holiday of Edith's life, and when she returned refreshed, she got a temporary position as a nurse in one of the clinics known as Queen's District Homes in industrial Manchester, a city in the Midlands. Many of her patients were poorly paid miners who had been injured in accidents down in the mines. These men adopted Edith as their favorite, just as the costermongers had at Shoreditch. Someone who knew of Edith's work with both groups gave her a title that everyone in Manchester picked up. Edith was known as "the poor man's Nightingale."

When the Matron at the Home fell ill, Edith was appointed to fill the job until she recovered. But Edith knew that whatever position she had at the Home was temporary. She could be out of work at any time. Since she was already forty-one years old, she worried about her future. Surely, she thought, she had shown enough talent as a nurse to win a steady position in a respected hospital. Over the years, she had applied for senior jobs at three or four hospitals, but she just missed out – the second choice on everyone's list. In Manchester, she was growing frustrated.

Then, unexpectedly, from a place she had never thought of, the perfect job was presented to her. It was to change Edith's life.

GARFIELD COUNTY
LIBRARIES

Checkout Receipt

08/29/2016

Parachute Branch Library
Need to renew?
970-285-9870
www.gcpld.org

TITLE   **Silent in an evil time : the**

BARCODE   **1220004039134**

DUE DATE   **09-19-16 00:00AM**

...ES CHARGE

D r. Antoine Depage of Brussels envied England's nursing system. A surgeon who ranked among the finest in Europe, Depage was brilliant and obstinate, and did not suffer fools gladly. Among the fools, in his opinion, were Belgium's nurses. Catholic nuns provided the care in the country's hospitals, and though the nuns had the best of intentions, their skills belonged in the dark ages of nursing, before Florence Nightingale brought enlightenment to the profession.

Dr. Depage was determined to raise Belgian nursing standards. He wanted his nurses to match the levels in care and knowledge of those in England. As a start, he decided to open Belgium's first training clinic. One thing that Depage insisted on for the new clinic was a Matron who had

Dr. Antoine Depage of Brussels was often difficult and demanding, but he was a medical pioneer and visionary. Not only did he open the first institution in Belgium to train nurses, but he had the foresight to hire Edith as the first Matron. (The Royal London Hospital Archives)

three qualifications: She must be English; she must speak fluent French; and she must have taken her training at one of England's great hospitals.

A young Brussels housewife named Marguerite Graux knew the very person who could meet each of Depage's requirements. Marguerite's maiden name was François. She was the oldest of the four François children in the household where Edith had served as governess from 1890 to 1895. The children never lost touch with their dear Edith Cavell, and Marguerite knew all about Edith's nursing career. She praised Edith to her mother-in-law, Madame Charles Graux, who happened to be president of the Ladies Committee that was helping Dr. Depage in launching his teaching clinic.

Among the upper classes, Brussels seemed a small town where everybody knew everybody else. The François, Graux, and Depage families moved in the same social circles, and through the connections, Dr. Depage soon learned all about Edith. He offered her the Matron's job. Edith was surprised and ecstatic, and in the middle of September 1907, she arrived in Brussels to take up her position at Dr. Depage's pioneering clinic.

—

Depage opened the clinic in four adjoining three-story houses on Rue de la Culture, in the Brussels suburb of Ixelles. It was only a short walk from the medical clinic where he carried on his practice. Edith and Dr. Depage assigned the houses to different uses. Number 143 became the living quarters for the nurses in training. Number 145 was divided into wards of five beds each, plus six single rooms for private patients. Number 147 underwent conversion into an operating theater and lecture rooms, in addition to providing beds for patients. Number 149 included wards on the upper stories and Edith's rooms on the ground floor. She had a small office and an even smaller reception room at the front; a kitchen, a sitting room, and a bedroom at the back.

Since Edith's responsibilities as Matron left her little free time, she

The clinic in Brussels, where Edith served as Matron for eight years, occupied four adjoining houses on Rue de la Culture. Her office and living quarters were on the ground floor of number 149. (The Royal London Hospital Archives)

hired a maid to look after the domestic chores at 149. The stocky middle-aged maid was named Marie – no record survives of her surname – and she was the kind of hard worker that Edith appreciated. Marie was German. Seven years later, once the First World War had broken out, Marie's presence in the clinic would become a major problem for Edith. The question of Marie and her loyalties would cost her many sleepless nights.

———

In October 1907, while Edith was still figuring out how to run the clinic, five young women enrolled, becoming the clinic's first trainees. Edith felt great pride in welcoming them to the new facility. These five, and all the other women who soon followed, signed up for five years of training. The first three years were to be spent attending lectures and nursing patients who came to the clinic, and in the final two years, the nurses were to be sent out as working student nurses in Belgian hospitals and private homes. At the end of the five years, the clinic would present the graduating nurses with diplomas, which qualified them for nursing positions in medical institutions throughout the country.

The clinic thrived from the start. Each year brought more young women keen to learn about nursing under Matron Cavell. By 1912, sixty nurses were at different stages of training. Besides Belgium, they came from France, the Netherlands, Switzerland, Germany, and even England.

"The Belgian school of nursing has been an entire success," Dr. Depage reported in a speech to the International Congress of Nurses in Cologne, Germany, in 1912. Then he listed all the places in Belgium where Cavell-trained nurses provided services: three hospitals, three private nursing homes, twenty-four communal schools, and thirteen kindergartens. Depage's speech drew a rousing ovation.

—

Edith ran a happy clinic. She set high standards, and at times, she could be severe in enforcing them. Like Eva Luckes at the London, Edith cracked down on nurses when they flirted with the doctors who treated the clinic's patients. This was a rule that puzzled the European nurses, who thought of themselves as more sophisticated than the English in matters of the heart. But the nurses found little else to complain about in the generous atmosphere that Edith created around the clinic.

The smart uniforms, which Edith helped to design, set the tone. The nurses wore blue cotton dresses, with long skirts and long sleeves. White aprons went over the dresses, and the caps were white and perky in a style called Sister Dora. These uniforms were a big leap forward from the dark and heavy robes that the nursing sisters wore in Belgium's hospitals. Edith

*Edith and her staff of senior nurses at the Brussels clinic wore plain but appealing
uniforms. Such smart outfits were previously unknown in Belgium's hospitals.*
(The Royal London Hospital Archives)

said in a speech that the difference in clothing was "a contrast of the
unhygienic past with the enlightened present."

Edith never missed a chance to pass along a piece of her personal phi-
losophy to the nurses. Once, during a lecture – Edith was a clear and
enthusiastic teacher – a spider crawled across the floor. A student nurse
raised a foot to crush it. Edith stopped her. "A woman does not take life,"
Edith said. "She gives it."

The tea parties were another custom that Edith adopted from Eva
Luckes. Luckes gave them every week for her nurses at the London, and
so did Edith in Brussels. Luckes invited the young women into her sitting
room, where she poured cups of tea and kept the conversation lively.
Edith went a step further. She joined the nurses in their rooms, in the
house at 143, for musical evenings. A piano was installed in the nurses'

quarters, and when enough of the young woman were off duty, they gathered at the piano to sing and play. Edith joined in, and none of the nurses felt awkward in their Matron's company. Clara Bohme, one of the first five nurses to join the clinic, said, "We were more like a family than anything else."

—

Edith kept two dogs as pets – one a Belgian sheepdog named Jackie and the other a mutt named Don, both born in 1909. Don died about six years later, while Jackie lived much longer. Edith had taken Jackie in as a stray, and he became his mistress' devoted companion. Later, in the time of Edith's work with the escape organization, Jackie accompanied her whenever she left the clinic on risky errands. Edith thought the Germans would never imagine that a middle-aged woman walking her dog could be up to anything suspicious.

A stray of an entirely different sort that Edith took in in 1912 was a tall attractive Englishwoman in her twenties, named Grace Jemmett. Jemmett came from a well-to-do family, but she had grown addicted to morphine as the result of treatment that went wrong for a nervous disorder. She couldn't stay away from the drug, and one of the many doctors who had no success in treating her was the man who married Edith's sister Lillian. He was Longworth Wainwright of St. Thomas' Hospital in London, and he had the idea that Edith's clinic might be the right place for Jemmett to get off morphine. She moved to Brussels, where Edith's best efforts couldn't help the young woman shake her addiction. Nevertheless, Edith kept Jemmett at the clinic for years, giving her a bedroom and Edith's own personal care.

Jemmett could be a handful. She stayed in bed for long periods, and, at other times, she wandered around the clinic smoking cigarettes. Edith showed patience that was so saintly, it was almost beyond imagining. She hid the clinic's supply of morphine and personally regulated the young woman's drug taking. Under Edith's guidance, Jemmett often made a charming companion, but when something upset Jemmett, she took to her bed and to her morphine.

—

In her years as Matron, Edith went on holiday each July to visit her family and friends in Norfolk. On most trips, she took Grace Jemmett. Edith's mother didn't like Jemmett. She considered her morphine addiction sinful, but more than that, Mrs. Cavell was jealous of the hours that Edith spent on Jemmett. It was time that the possessive Mrs. Cavell thought Edith should be devoting to her mother, rather than to an erratic drug addict.

In June 1910, the Reverend Frederick Cavell died at age eighty-five. He was buried in the cemetery beside his church in Swardeston. After his death, Mrs. Cavell moved to a little house in Norwich, where she had the help of a maid. Edith tried to persuade her mother to make a home at the clinic in Brussels. Mrs. Cavell resisted until early 1914, when she visited Brussels for several weeks. She discovered that she couldn't stand the place. The French language confused her, and Grace Jemmett got on her nerves. Before the end of the winter, Mrs. Cavell was gone from Brussels, back to her little house in Norwich.

—

When Edith took her annual holiday in July that year, a trip which, to Mrs. Cavell's relief, did not include Grace Jemmett, Edith had mixed feelings. Since 1912, a plan to build a clinic that would replace the four overcrowded houses had been in the works, and now construction was going ahead at a promising rate. The new clinic on Rue Brussels, about a kilometer from Rue de la Culture, would combine everything that was up to date in medical care. Edith consulted Dr. Depage and an architect in planning the building, and she knew that it would attract more student nurses, who would receive more complete training. The prospect thrilled her.

At the same time, Edith was uneasy. There was speculation about a war involving almost all of Europe, which left her concerned about the year ahead. Every other citizen in Brussels who was paying attention to events felt the same way. Relations among European countries were disintegrating, and war was an increasing possibility. When Edith went on vacation in early July – she always liked to be in Norwich for her mother's birthday on July 6 – she left instructions with a senior nurse, Millicent White. If the news in Brussels suggested war, then White must send a telegram of warning to Edith.

Chapter Six

THE WAR TO END ALL WARS

I n the early years of the twentieth century, Europe's five most powerful nations were Britain, France, Germany, Russia, and the Austro-Hungarian Empire. While all were rich in resources and industry, each nation had doubts and complaints about the others. Germany was jealous of Britain's mighty navy. France wished it had an army as large and disciplined as Germany's. Russia spent its wealth in building a military with bigger guns and stronger fortifications, all in the interests of not looking second-rate in comparison with the others. Germany objected that it had far fewer colonies in Asia and Africa than either Britain or France had. The British and French were growing more prosperous from their colonization of both continents, and the Germans considered their monopoly to be unfair.

The decisive battles of the First World War were fought in the trenches of northeastern France and in parts of Belgium. Millions of soldiers on both sides, Allied and German, died of gunfire and gas attacks before Germany surrendered on November 11, 1918. (The Toronto Reference Library)

Austria-Hungary, the least of the five powers, felt it received no respect from any of the others except Germany. The population of the Austro-Hungarian Empire included groups of citizens divided by a dozen languages and five religions. The German Austrians, led by the prolific Habsburg family, dominated the empire for centuries, even though they were out-numbered by the Serbians and the other Slavic peoples who made up a large and unhappy subgroup within the empire.

Europe was officially at peace, but it was a nervous peace. None of the countries said they wanted war. All tried to manage workable diplomatic relations with the rest, and France and Russia maintained an alliance that had lasted for decades. Still, the five powers kept themselves armed just in case someone started a war. By "someone," France, Russia, and Britain had Germany in mind, the country that was involved in more differences of opinion than anybody else. To the others, Germany seemed to bargain with a chip on its shoulder, and by 1914, German leaders were signaling that they might challenge the rest of the powers at any moment.

—

In June 1914, Austria-Hungary held its army's annual practice battle in the empire's province of Bosnia. Archduke Franz Ferdinand of the Habsburg family arrived in Bosnia on June 25 as the senior official in charge of supervising the battle. The archduke had the best of credentials; he was inspector general of the army and nephew of Austria-Hungary's Emperor Franz Josef.

When the army finished its practice battle three days later, the arch-duke and his wife were driven many miles in a procession of cars for a ceremonial visit to Bosnia's governor. The governor's residence was in the city of Sarajevo. Lying in wait for the archduke in the city's streets were five young Austrian citizens of Serbian background who had armed them-selves with bombs and pistols. The five belonged to an extremist group of

In June 1914, when Serbian nationalists assassinated Archduke Franz Ferdinand of the Austro-Hungarian Empire (above right), the stage was set for the outbreak of the First World War. The man in the lavish sideburns striding in front of the archduke is Franz Joseph, the Austro-Hungarian emperor. (The Toronto Reference Library)

Nationalist Serbs who resented the rule of the Habsburgs. They intended to assassinate the archduke.

As the royal motorcade entered Sarajevo, an assassin threw a bomb at the archduke's car. The bomb bounced off its target and exploded under the next car in the line, wounding an officer. The motorcade proceeded on its way, giving no sign of panic. Forty-five minutes later, still on the way to the governor's house, the chauffeur driving the archduke made a wrong turn. He realized his mistake right away, but while he was backing up and turning around, he came to a stop in front of a man who was standing on the sidewalk. By a horrible coincidence, the man was another of the five Serbian assassins. He pulled out his pistol and shot the archduke and his wife. They died on the spot. The Serb killer was arrested.

—

The archduke's shocking assassination set off a chain of reactions among Europe's five powers. Austria-Hungary's Habsburgs were eager to declare war on the tiny kingdom of Serbia, which supported the Serb radicals within the Austro-Hungarian Empire. But the Habsburgs wanted assurance that Germany would help them in their fight. The Germans encouraged the Habsburgs to go ahead with an invasion of Serbia, whenever they were ready. Russia, long devoted to the Serbs, announced its support of Serbia in any war that was brought against the little kingdom. France already had a treaty with Russia that required each country to come to the aid of the other if Germany invaded one of the two. And both France and England were joined under an ancient treaty, in which they promised to protect Belgium if the Germans violated the country's neutrality.

By late July, after a month of bickering among all the nations, both Russia and Germany threatened to mobilize their armies at any minute. Diplomats from England and France warned the Germans and the Russians of the trigger effect of mobilization – if one country took up arms, then all the others would soon do the same. Neither Russia nor Germany appeared to appreciate the danger.

The Germans were feeling bold. In their opinion, they had a tremendous military scheme in place. It was called the Schlieffen Plan, named after the man who designed it, Field Marshal Alfred von Schlieffen, once chief of the German Great General Staff. The minutely detailed plan committed seven-eighths of the German army to a massive assault on France. As far as Germany was concerned, the Schlieffen Plan guaranteed that the Germans would capture Paris and defeat France in exactly forty-two days. After that, the German army would turn to Russia and give it the same beating.

But Germany didn't pull the first trigger. That role was filled by the Austro-Hungarian Empire. On Tuesday, July 28, still fuming over the murder of Archduke Franz Ferdinand, Austria-Hungary declared war on Serbia. Two days later, Serbia's protector, Russia, announced that it was mobilizing its army. On the following afternoon, July 31, Germany dispatched telegrams to both Russia and Russia's good friend France, advising that Germany would mobilize its own army unless the Russians promised to suspend their war measures. The Germans demanded an answer from the Russians within twelve hours.

—

Millicent White, the senior nurse at Edith Cavell's clinic, took the events in Germany and Russia as a signal of big trouble ahead. Early on Saturday morning, August 1, she sent a telegram to Edith in Norwich, warning her that war seemed to be on the way. That afternoon, while Edith was weeding her mother's garden, a messenger delivered the telegram. When Edith read it, Mrs. Cavell begged her not to return to Brussels.

"My duty is with my nurses," Edith said.

—

On Saturday evening, Russia told Germany that it was rejecting the German demand to stop the mobilization of the Russian army. Germany's response was to announce that it, too, was mobilizing its army and to declare war on Russia.

The next day, Sunday, Germany delivered an ultimatum to Belgium – unless the Belgians allowed the German army to march through the country without interference, Germany would treat it as an enemy. The

Schlieffen Plan depended on a quick German passage to France by way of Belgium, and Germany told the Belgians that they had twenty-four hours to make up their minds. As everybody recognized, the German demands indicated that Germany was about to launch its war against France.

—

Edith Cavell took the Sunday-evening boat across the English Channel to Ostend, on the Belgian coast, where she caught a train that would reach Brussels early Monday morning.

—

In Brussels, King Albert I of Belgium summoned his military leaders to the Senate chamber late on Sunday night. For hours, past midnight and into Monday morning, the men discussed Belgium's answer to the German ultimatum. Albert, an honorable man, didn't want Belgium to be the cause of a full-scale European war. On the other hand, Germany's bullying made him furious. The answer that Albert and his generals drew up said, in the most dignified language, that Belgium would oppose any attack on its borders. A document with the answer was delivered to the German legation in Brussels at seven o'clock on Monday morning. That was just about the time when Edith arrived back in the city to take charge of her clinic.

—

As six of the clinic's nurses in training were Germans, Edith's first order of business was to get them out of Belgium. None of the European countries had yet fired a shot, but Edith knew that Brussels could soon become a dangerous spot for the six young German women. She wasn't worried about her German maid, Marie, who was older and could handle herself in Brussels. The risk was different for the youthful and inexperienced nurses. Edith took the six to the train station and saw them off to their fatherland.

When she returned to the clinic, Edith began preparations to care for soldiers wounded in battle. If Germany invaded Belgium, Edith expected that the Belgian army would need all the hospital beds in the city to look after casualties from the war front. She was also certain that the clinic would come under the rules and regulations of the International Committee of the Red Cross when war broke out. This meant that Edith and her nurses would be called on to treat the wounded from every country, both allies and enemies, both Belgian and German. The clinic had to be ready to play its part.

—

Later on Monday, Germany pushed Europe to the brink of all-out war. Confident that the Schlieffen Plan would bring an early victory, the Germans declared war on France. A few hours after the declaration, when Germany's ultimatum to Belgium expired, German troops massed along the border between the two countries. In the darkness of early Tuesday morning, the Germans crossed into Belgium.

With Germany's invasion of Belgium, the old treaty signed by France and England guaranteeing Belgian neutrality came into effect. By midnight, Tuesday, August 4, Britain was at war with Germany. So were France and Russia. The countries of the British Empire, Canada among them, declared war on Germany, and within a week, Austria-Hungary joined Germany in the war against England and all of the other Allied nations.

—

The war had begun. Everybody called it the Great War because it involved all of Europe's powers. It was expected to settle rivalries that had existed over the past century. For this reason, it was also called the War to End All Wars. It would become known, finally and officially, under a third name, the First World War, in 1943, four years after the start of the Second World War.

Under all its names, the war lasted from the summer of 1914 until late in 1918, and it didn't come near to ending all wars. But it was the most deadly war in history until then. Millions from both sides died in the fighting. The overwhelming majority of deaths resulted from soldiers shelling and shooting at one another in massive artillery and infantry battles. But among the others who gave their lives were men and women who never picked up a gun. Edith Cavell was one of them.

OPPOSITE: *The men in the spiked helmets are German soldiers posing in front of the beautiful town hall in Brussels, which the Germans occupied in August 1914.* (The Royal London Hospital Archives)

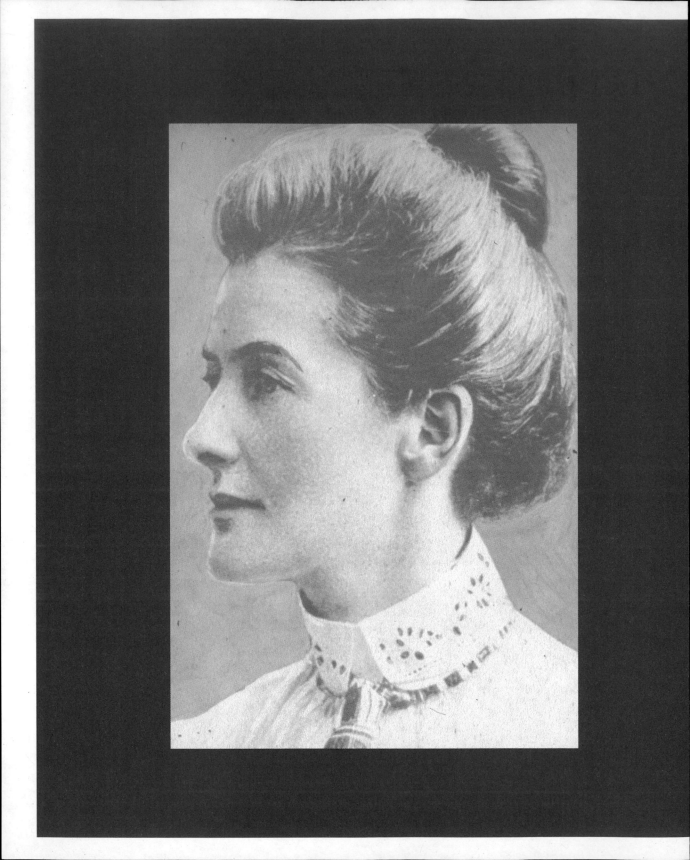

Chapter Seven

EDITH'S FATEFUL CHOICE

E dith was astonished at how quiet it was in Brussels during August 1914. To the east, the small Belgian army in its old-fashioned uniforms, equipped with out-of-date guns, was doing its best to slow the German powerhouse. The Germans expected no opposition at all, and they grew impatient at the Belgian resistance. In several villages, they took out their anger on the local people. The German soldiers lined up men, women, and children in the main square of each village and shot them. Reports of these horrors reached Brussels, shocking everyone. But few soldiers wounded in the battles had yet turned up at the clinic. Edith and her nurses had little work on their hands.

The Germans needed three weeks to conquer Belgium. During those weeks, Edith told her English nurses that they still had time to get back to the safety of England. All refused. Edith told the same thing to Grace

At the outbreak of the First World War, Edith had developed the assurance and courage she needed to take up her dangerous work against the invading German troops. (The Royal London Hospital Archives)

Jemmett. Not wanting to be separated from Edith's protection, Jemmett chose to stay. But she went to her bed and remained there for several weeks. As for Edith, it never occurred to her to leave for England. Whenever anybody brought up the subject, she replied with the same answer she had given her mother – her duty was with the clinic and her nurses. The clinic was now under the auspices of the Red Cross. That made little difference in the way Edith ran it, but as Matron at a Red Cross institution, Edith's status allowed her to remain in Brussels, even after the Germans occupied the city.

The occupation took place on August 20, when the German army marched into the middle of Brussels. No fighting in the city preceded its arrival; all of the battles were out in the countryside and in the smaller towns. Twenty thousand German soldiers in their gray uniforms paraded to Brussels' town hall. They took down the bright tricolor flag of Belgium and replaced it with the German black, white, and red. The city had become occupied territory.

—

Brussels turned into a duller, darker, more anxious place. Many kinds of food ran short, and people were afraid that their supply of coal for the coming winter would be cut back. The use of electricity at night was restricted, and Germany allowed no Belgian newspapers to be published, leaving Edith and everybody else unaware of events in Belgium and the world beyond. The Germans imposed martial law on the conquered country. All citizens were required to carry identification papers. German soldiers could stop them at any time to check name, address, and other personal details. If anything seemed fishy, the Germans dragged the poor citizen off to jail.

—

It was three days after the occupation of Brussels that the German army fought a fierce battle against the British near Mons, a town thirty-five kilometers south of the capital. Sticking to the Schlieffen Plan, the Germans had driven toward the border between Belgium and France. When they reached Mons, they discovered that eighty thousand troops from the British Expeditionary Force, which had just arrived from England, were dug in for thirty kilometers along the Condé-Mons Canal, waiting for the Germans to show up.

At noon on August 23, the British opened fire. Their soldiers included veterans from the Boer War of a dozen years earlier. These men were crafty fighters, and they were equipped with fine new Lee-Enfield rifles, which shot at the amazing rate of fifteen rounds a minute. The British blasted away and brought the German advance to a halt. They killed or wounded five thousand German soldiers, while suffering just fifteen hundred casualties themselves.

But the BEF's generals, knowing that the German army was still far stronger than theirs, never intended the battle at Mons to last more than a few hours. The day before, on August 22, the French army was badly beaten by the Germans in a battle at Charleroi, a village not far from Mons. French soldiers went into an immediate retreat, and on the morning of August 24, the BEF joined the French in falling back into France.

One result of the retreat was that hundreds of British soldiers were left behind enemy lines. In the speed and confusion of the fallback, many soldiers missed the orders to move out. Others couldn't keep up, or were slowed by wounds, or were pointed in the wrong direction. These soldiers were caught in the rear of the German advance, and their only choice was to go into hiding in the Belgian countryside and in the thick French forests.

—

The Schlieffen Plan, which promised the capture of Paris within forty-two days, came close to succeeding. Before the fortieth day of the war,

Germany's soldiers needed only another day or two of fighting to make their way into Paris. The French were so concerned that they prepared to blow up one of the city's most renowned structures, the Eiffel Tower, which served as the transmitting station for French army communications. But at this crucial moment, the German army weakened under the strain of almost six weeks of marching and warfare. The French and British tightened their resistance against the flagging Germans. Paris was saved, and the war settled into a stalemate of fighting in the trenches of northern and eastern France. Neither side made much headway for the rest of 1914 and all of 1915.

—

Through September and October 1914, Edith was frustrated at the lack of activity around her clinic in Brussels. "We are actually doing no work among the wounded," she wrote in a letter to her sister Florence. Even in the occupied city, Edith discovered ways of getting a letter to the outside world. "Everything is out of our hands at the present," she went on. "The enemy have made their own arrangements."

Edith and her nurses filled the hours by sewing and knitting clothes for Belgian refugees from towns and villages that the Germans had destroyed. They worked on long-term plans for a children's Christmas party. And from time to time, they treated wounded German soldiers, under the supervision of German doctors. Edith continued her usual training of student nurses, though there were fewer of them in wartime and almost all were Belgian. The senior nurse, Millicent White, and some of the other nurses were often sent to care for the wounded in hospitals throughout Brussels.

But life on Rue de la Culture was slow for Edith. She was used to being of service to her patients and her nurses. For now, she had few of either, and the empty days filled her with aggravation. What she couldn't know was that an adventure was unfolding south of Brussels that would wipe the dullness from her life.

—

Dudley Boger and Fred Meachin, two men whose names would soon become familiar to Edith, were members of the British Expeditionary Force that fought at Mons. Boger, forty-nine years old, came from a family with a long record of military and naval service. His own career was distinguished, and by 1914, he held the rank of colonel and commanded the 1st Battalion of the Cheshire Regiment. When the war broke out, Boger told his wife that he expected to be killed in action, or taken prisoner of war, or appointed to the rank of general. He was right about one of the three. Fred Meachin, in his twenties, was a noncommissioned officer and served as a sergeant with the 1st Cheshires. He was affable, brave, and devoted to his commanding officer, Colonel Boger.

On the morning of August 24, as the BEF retreated from Mons, the Cheshires' assignment was to fight a rearguard action against the Germans, stalling the enemy long enough for the other British troops to get further down the road into France. It was a necessary but hopeless battle. The Germans killed dozens of the Cheshires' soldiers and wounded many more. Fred Meachin was one of the first to be hit – once by a bullet, then by a piece of shrapnel that ricocheted off a tree. The hits knocked Meachin unconscious, and he lay in a field for hours. Dudley Boger took even more shots than Meachin. He was wounded in the hand, the side, and the right foot. Unable to walk, he crawled to a nearby house. To his unpleasant surprise, the house turned out to be a headquarters for German officers, who took Boger prisoner.

The Germans transported him to the nearby village of Wiheries, where they had converted a convent into a temporary hospital. German doctors looked after Boger's wounds, but his foot was badly smashed and needed surgery, which the temporary hospital wasn't equipped to carry out. While Boger was recuperating, Fred Meachin stumbled into the convent, wounded and looking for his commanding officer. The Germans made Meachin a prisoner and put him to bed.

"I don't intend to stay here for long," Boger said to Meachin.

"Neither do I, sir," Meachin answered.

—

After a month, near the end of September, Boger led an escape from the convent hospital that included Meachin and six or seven other British soldiers. The escape wasn't difficult since the Germans posted only one sentry to watch the prisoner patients. While the sentry was eating his breakfast, the soldiers climbed the wall around the convent and hurried off.

Boger and Meachin were taken in by Albert Libiez, a Mons lawyer who had a house in Wiheries. Libiez was a member of a secret group of Belgians and French that was helping English soldiers to escape. The group, still in the early period of its organization, made up plans on the fly – playing things by instinct and hoping for the best. Libiez hid Boger and Meachin in the loft of a shed, in the garden behind his house.

With Libiez's help, Boger and Meachin worked out disguises to enable them to move among the German occupiers. Boger's disguise came easily, since he spoke excellent French. He let his beard grow long and dressed himself in rough clothes, topped off by the black hat and floppy tie that all Belgian factory workers wore. In this outfit, Boger could pass as a local factory hand. Meachin presented a tougher problem. He had no French, and because he looked young and healthy, German soldiers were likely to ask why he wasn't in the Belgian army. The dilemma was solved by stuffing rolls of cloth under the shoulders at the back of his jacket. When Meachin stooped over, he looked like a hunchback. He put a woeful expression on his face, and presented himself as an unfortunate soul whom no German would think to stop and question.

—

Meanwhile, in Brussels, Edith continued to experience conflicting emotions. She was disheartened that the clinic wasn't busy enough at its real job of training nurses, and she felt tense over the course of the war. Like other citizens in Belgium, she was apprehensive at the prospect of German rule throughout Europe. Certainly, at this stage in events, it never crossed Edith's mind that she might take a role in opposing the German occupiers. She had no idea that a secret organization was already beginning its work in sheltering British soldiers in the south of Belgium. Nor would she have imagined in her wildest dreams that she might become part of such a valiant organization.

—

For weeks, Colonel Boger and Sergeant Meachin hid out in Belgian barns and attics, and bluffed their way through two tricky encounters with German soldiers. Then Herman Capiau, an engineer from Mons who worked in the secret organization, offered to guide them to Brussels. Capiau equipped the two with fake identity papers, and on the first day of November, he accompanied them aboard the train from Mons to Brussels. Along the way, a group of young German soldiers got on the train. They were in high spirits, laughing and joking, and when they spotted Meachin, they made fun of the silent hunchback. Meachin almost lashed out at the Germans, which would have given away his identity. Fortunately for Meachin, he kept his temper in check.

In Brussels, Capiau hadn't arranged for a house where Boger and Meachin could stay. He led them to a list of addresses, but no one would agree to hide the English soldiers – it was too dangerous. Capiau tried Dr. Antoine Depage's house. Marie Depage, the doctor's wife, was the only one at home. The opposite of her prickly husband, Marie was a sunny and charming women who had a warm friendship with Edith. She told Capiau that she, the wife of a prominent Brussels surgeon, couldn't risk helping Boger and Meachin, but as an afterthought, she suggested that he take the two to Edith's clinic. The three men made their way to Rue de la Culture.

—

At eight o'clock that evening, Capiau knocked on Edith's door at number 149. In the reception room, the senior nurse, Millicent White, was absorbed in reading the *Times*, an October 13 issue of the London newspaper that had been smuggled into the clinic. Afraid that whoever was knocking might be German, White slid the newspaper out of sight. Edith's maid, Marie, answered the door and showed Capiau and the disguised English soldiers into the Matron's office, where Edith was doing paperwork.

Five or six minutes was all the time Edith needed to listen to the men's story and make the most important decision of her life: She offered Boger and Meachin a place in the clinic. With this simple act, she became part of the secret organization helping the Allies against the Germans.

Capiau was relieved to be rid of the responsibility for Boger and Meachin. As he left the clinic for the train station, Edith introduced the two English soldiers to Millicent White. She told White to put Boger and Meachin in beds on the second floor of number 147, the house next door. White was to get the men a meal and treat the colonel's wounded foot.

"Oh, yes," Edith said, "and be sure to give Colonel Boger and Sergeant Meachin a beer from the kitchen."

When Boger was comfortable in bed, he read the clinic's copy of the October 13 *Times*. The newspaper listed England's casualties in the

Marie Depage, wife of Dr. Antoine Depage, sometimes helped out at the clinic. But she was more effective behind the scenes, raising money to build the new clinic. In May 1915, she was returning from a fund-raising trip to the United States when her ship was sunk by a German submarine. (The Royal London Hospital Archives)

fighting in Belgium and France. Running down the names on the list, Boger felt suddenly weak. His brother, Captain R.A. Boger of the Royal Engineers and the Royal Flying Corps, was missing in action.

—

Boger and Meachin stayed in the clinic for two weeks, cared for by Edith and her English nurses. From the start, the nurses were in on Edith's decision to help Boger, Meachin, and all the British soldiers who came later. None of them ever backed out of the mission, and none betrayed Edith.

Colonel Boger's foot had become infected. If it got worse, the foot would have to be amputated. Edith used her contacts to find a surgeon who would agree to operate on Boger without needing to know the colonel's identity. The operation saved the foot. Meachin had an easier time. In his hunchback outfit, he often went shopping with Edith to practice mingling with Germans in the city. As soon as Boger's foot healed, Edith would arrange help for the two soldiers to cross into Holland.

The Germans, who were living in all parts of Brussels, didn't notice anything suspicious going on at the clinic. But neighbors on Rue de la Culture began to ask questions about the hunchback and the man with the limp. As a precaution, Edith convinced an English friend in another section of the city to shelter Boger and Meachin until they were ready to leave for Holland. For the escape, Meachin was to wear a different disguise. Someone brought him a dress and a girdle. Meachin said he'd rather be taken prisoner than dress up as a woman. Instead, he agreed to disguise himself in fisherman's clothes.

—

Equipped with Edith's careful directions, Boger and Meachin set off separately toward Holland, agreeing to meet in a town just across the Dutch border. Even with his impeccable French, Boger caught the eye of a German officer before he got out of Brussels. He had stepped into a bar for a drink, and the German, sensing something not quite Belgian about Boger, took him to army headquarters for questioning. Boger spent the next four years in a German prisoner-of-war camp. One of the three predictions he'd made to his wife had come true.

Wearing his fisherman's disguise, Meachin, too, came close to getting nabbed by the Germans. A real Belgian fisherman, hired by Edith to guide Meachin to the border, panicked when the two stopped at a restaurant and found it filled with German soldiers. The guide went back out the door and rushed away, never to be seen again. From his shopping excursions with Edith, Meachin was accustomed to handling himself among the enemy. He kept his cool in the restaurant and attracted no stares or questions. But he was now on his own in occupied territory, not sure of the best route to Holland. He slept one night in a pigsty and another in a woodshed. He lived on a diet of raw turnips. By luck, he met a man who was sympathetic to the Allied cause. The man changed Meachin's disguise from fisherman to turnip picker, and led him to the frontier.

Meachin and his new friend found a spot to cross into Holland that seemed to be clear of German guards. They checked both ways, then set out at a trot toward the other side of the border. What neither noticed was a lone German sentry. The sentry raised his rifle and fired at the backs of the fleeing men. The shots flew wide. Running for their lives, Meachin and his guide speeded up until they were clear of the border.

When Meachin returned to England, his army superiors thought he must have deserted his regiment. What else explained the three months he had been on the loose in Belgium? The army brass intended to send Meachin to a court-martial. But they finally believed the sergeant's remarkable story of Edith Cavell, the secret organization, and Meachin's dash for freedom. After a short holiday with his wife and two small daughters, Meachin rejoined his regiment and fought again for the Cheshires in Europe. He survived the war and lived to a good age.

—

Colonel Dudley Boger and Sergeant Fred Meachin were the first British soldiers who approached Edith for help in escaping the Germans. Guided by members of the secret network, hundreds more came to Edith's clinic with the same request. A few of these men were captured, as Boger had been. But most of them went free in the way that Meachin had, and like him, they lived to fight on against the enemy. With Boger and Meachin, Edith's heroic work had begun.

Château de BELLIGNIES

Chapter Eight

THE SECRET NETWORK

P rince Reginald de Croy and Princess Marie de Croy lived in a château as grand as a castle. The prince and princess were a middle-aged brother and sister who came from an established family related to royalty all over Europe. The château, called Bellignies, stood just across the border in France, a few kilometers from Mons. That placed it close to the forests where British soldiers from the battle at Mons and French soldiers from the fighting at Charleroi were hiding to avoid capture by the Germans. Prince Reginald and Princess Marie were intensely patriotic, and they decided to make Bellignies a refuge for the Allied soldiers. They would take in the men, give them food and shelter, and put them on the path back to their own armies.

—

The château was the home of Prince Reginald and Princess Marie de Croy, a brother and sister who were key members of the secret organization of French and Belgian citizens who worked with Edith to help soldiers escape from the Germans. The prince and princess hid many fleeing British, French, and Belgian soldiers inside the beautiful château. (The Royal London Hospital Archives)

Part of the château consisted of an ancient tower that hadn't been used for centuries. In medieval times, the de Croy family imprisoned their enemies in the tower. Its walls were nine feet thick, and no sound could be heard from the inside. The prince and princess thought the abandoned tower was a perfect place to conceal British and French soldiers. From September 1914 until midway through 1915, it became the hideout for hundreds of men on their way out of the country. The Germans grew suspicious of the de Croys, but they never caught a hidden British or French soldier in the château, no matter how often they showed up to search.

On one sudden German raid, Princess Marie's swift action saved a dozen British soldiers from capture. At the time the Germans arrived, the soldiers happened to be chatting with the princess in one of Bellignies' drawing rooms. Princess Marie jumped up from her chair and pulled back a secret panel in the drawing-room wall. The panel opened an entrance to a hidden passageway. The princess pushed the soldiers into the dusty inner chamber, then slid the panel back into place.

In the drawing room, Princess Marie lay down on a sofa, covering her legs with a rug and placing a cloth over her forehead. She was pretending to be sick in the hope that her "illness" would discourage the Germans from spending much time in the room. The plan worked. The Germans concentrated on searching the château's other rooms. None of them spotted the secret panel leading to the passageway, and they all soon left Bellignies empty-handed.

—

Prince Reginald and Princess Marie made contact with other men and women in the area who were assisting the British and French soldiers. Together they formed a network to smuggle soldiers out of occupied territory. Louise Thuliez was prominent in the group, a schoolteacher from the city of Lille in northern France who was on holiday in a village near

Bellignies when war broke out. She stayed on to help hide soldiers from the Germans and steer them to shelter at the de Croy castle. Thuliez soon became one of the network's valiant figures.

Princess Marie snapped the photographs of the soldiers that were needed for their fake identity papers. Like the princess, everybody in the network contributed different talents. A pharmacist named Georges Derveau, who owned a shop in a village close to Mons, developed Princess Marie's photographs. Auguste Joly, a husky and fearless miner from Wiheries, had two specialties. He was resourceful at rounding up clothes to disguise the English soldiers, and he joined Prince Reginald in handling the tense business of guiding the soldiers from Mons to Brussels.

People in the network came from every background. Jeanne de Belleville was a well-to-do countess with a country home close to Bellignies. Désiré Richez lived in Wiheries, and, like Auguste Joly, he worked as a low-paid miner. Both took key roles in the network. Countess de Belleville began her association with the organization to help her young nephew join the French army, but she stayed on to assist countless other British and French soldiers to evade the Germans. Désiré Richez, who had a wife and two children, worked wonders in concealing one English soldier in his small home for almost eight months. The soldier was Charlie Scott, a private from the Norfolk Regiment who suffered severe wounds to his chest in the fighting at Mons. Richez and his family treated Scott with the little medical equipment they owned, and they were ingenious in improvising a hiding spot for Scott when the Germans arrived on searching expeditions.

Richez, Countess de Belleville, the de Croys, and the others linked up with such people as Albert Libiez and Herman Capiau, the men who sheltered Colonel Boger and Sergeant Meachin. The secret network continued to grow, all of its members cooperating to protect British and French soldiers from the enemy. They developed routes to guide the soldiers from Mons and Bellignies to Brussels. As their work proceeded, the men and women in the secret network came to agree on the most reliable place in Brussels to deliver the escaping men. Without doubt, it was Edith Cavell's clinic.

—

Sergeant Jesse Tunmore belonged to the Norfolk Regiment. He was one of the soldiers who escaped with Colonel Boger from the convent hospital in Wiheries. For weeks he survived in the forest, until he had the good luck to meet Auguste Joly, the miner. Joly supplied Tunmore with food and clothes, and told him how to get to Edith in Brussels. Tunmore reached Rue de la Culture two days before Christmas 1914.

"How do I know you're really a British soldier?" Edith asked Tunmore. She was teasing. Tunmore should have realized that both he and Edith spoke English with the same distinctive Norfolk accent.

"Well," he said nervously, pointing to a picture on Edith's wall, "I recognize that that's a picture of Norwich Cathedral."

"You know Norwich, do you?" Edith said, with a smile. "I know Norwich too."

Tunmore relaxed.

Edith explained that the clinic was a wartime Red Cross institution, and for that reason, she and her nurses were caring for wounded German soldiers. It was essential that she keep Tunmore out of the Germans' sight. Edith led him to the clinic's cellar, where Tunmore joined two other British soldiers in hiding. Edith arranged for the nurses to bring him food, and she visited Tunmore and the others each day. Years later, Tunmore remembered Edith as "slim, quiet, kind in every way – and clever."

—

On Christmas Day, Edith served roast beef and plum pudding, from her mother's special recipe, to the soldiers in the cellar. Upstairs that

These brave English nurses posed for this photograph just as they left the London Hospital in the autumn of 1914. They were on their way to serve in British field hospitals in France during the war's early fighting and couldn't know what horrors lay in store. (The Royal London Hospital Archives)

evening, the clinic put on the children's Christmas party they had been planning for months. Thirty boys and girls and their parents gathered for food, gifts, carol singing, and a few hours when thoughts of the war were pushed aside.

A day or two later, Edith took a photo of Tunmore for a fake passport. Though she wasn't as expert at photography as Princess Marie de Croy, Edith owned an old box Kodak camera that she used for snapping pictures on her holidays. When the passport was ready, Tunmore was guided to the Dutch border, where he met disaster. A German guard pointed out to Tunmore something that neither he nor Edith had noticed: The passport was out of date. Staying calm, Tunmore nodded his apologies to the guard and made his way back to the clinic.

At 5:30 in the morning, a few days after New Year's, equipped with a properly dated passport, Tunmore started for the border once again. This time he was accompanied partway by Edith and her dog, Jackie. The new document passed the guard's inspection. Tunmore crossed into Holland. While he was there, he picked up what seemed a reliable tip about Germany's intentions to send a fleet of zeppelins to drop bombs on London. A zeppelin was a huge airship, with a cylinder shape and a covered frame that held gas cells. It could carry an impressive load of bombs. Tunmore's source even mentioned a date for the attack: January 19.

When he reached England, Tunmore passed on the information to his superiors. January 19 arrived, and by that day, the British had mounted special defenses around London. The zeppelins arrived on schedule, but fell back when the pilots couldn't penetrate the defenses. Needing to get rid of the bombs before they started the return trip across the English Channel, the zeppelins dropped their explosives on the nearest area they flew over. That was Norfolk, home county to Edith and Tunmore.

—

From mid-December 1914 to mid-January 1915, the clinic hid ten French soldiers, survivors of the battle at Charleroi, and twenty British soldiers that fought at Mons. The escaping men were coming so often and in such numbers that Edith needed to find other people in Brussels willing to take them in. One was her neighbor, a pharmacist named Louis Séverin. Another was an Irishwoman, Ada Bodart, who had married a Belgian and moved to Brussels. Bodart didn't hesitate to join the secret organization, even though her son Philippe, a slim pale fourteen-year-old, was put at risk.

Hiding the soldiers and recruiting others to do the same was only the first part of Edith's role. She entered even more deeply into the secret organization's work by lining up guides to accompany the soldiers to the

Dutch border. Some of the guides wanted money to cover their services and expenses, so Edith asked for donations from those who supported the organization's work. No one turned down an appeal from Edith.

A potential source of trouble that she needed to deal with, though, was the heavy traffic of men coming and going at the clinic. Edith was afraid that the arrivals and departures of guides might attract the Germans' notice. To solve the problem, she helped choose six locations around Brussels where the soldiers and their guides could meet, far from Rue de la Culture. Each rendezvous had to be in a public place – a corner where a man hanging around for a few minutes wouldn't draw suspicion. Edith didn't miss a trick in thinking up ways of avoiding the Germans. In a pinch, when no guides at all were available, Edith acted as guide herself. She filled whatever role needed filling.

—

In late January, a lance corporal named Doman from Britain's 9th Lancers and a private named Chapman from the 1st Cheshires arrived together at Edith's clinic. Georges Derveau, the pharmacist who developed Princess de Croÿ's photographs, had acted as their guide from Mons to Brussels. Like others in the organization, Derveau was branching out into other activities, even though that made him more vulnerable. Once Doman and Chapman reached Rue de la Culture, they were anxious to set off for the Dutch border. But Edith ran into delays in her hunt for a guide, and the days of waiting stretched into weeks.

One morning, when Doman was upstairs in one of the clinic's wards, a group of German soldiers arrived for an unannounced inspection tour. Edith whipped the fully dressed Doman into an empty bed and pulled the blankets up to his neck. Doman still had his boots on, so Edith fluffed the blankets over the bulge. She was using the same trick that would save Private Arthur Wood a few weeks later.

"This man is a Belgian from the countryside," Edith said, pointing to Doman as she spoke to the head of the German group. "He is suffering from severe rheumatic fever. A very serious condition."

The Germans backed away, went on to another ward, and soon departed.

Edith now realized she could no longer delay moving Doman and Chapman north to the border. She took them to the rectory of a Catholic priest who was friendly to her network. The priest assured her that he knew a guide for Doman and Chapman. He tore a card in two and gave half to Edith. He instructed her to go back to the clinic with the soldiers, but to bring them and her half of the card to a certain Brussels bar at a certain time two days later.

Edith followed the priest's instructions to the letter, accompanying Doman and Chapman to the bar by streetcar. They sat down at a table. Since neither soldier spoke French, Edith took charge of ordering three glasses of beer from the waiter. She placed her half of the card on the table. Trying their best to look nonchalant, Edith and the soldiers sipped the glasses of beer and glanced around the bar. It was filled with German soldiers. The passing minutes seemed like hours, but soon a Belgian man stopped at their table. A stranger to Edith, he studied the half card. Then he took the other half from his pocket and fit it to Edith's half. It was the sign Edith needed that this man was the guide.

The guide joined them in a beer, and for a few minutes, he and Edith chatted like a couple of old friends. The ability to play the part of an undercover agent seemed to come naturally to Edith – in a room of enemy soldiers, she didn't give the slightest outward show of fear. Finally, she said a gracious good-bye to the three men. She walked confidently past the German soldiers and out into the street.

After another beer, the guide left the bar with Doman and Chapman. A day later, the three attempted to cross the border, but German sentries manned the checkpoint at the frontier where they intended to cross. One sentry called out to them with a question, and when their answer didn't ring true, he fired warning shots over the men's heads. The three took off for the Dutch side of the frontier, running as fast as they had ever run in their lives. Their effort was so great that the muscles in Chapman's legs seized up. Doman grabbed one of Chapman's arms, the guide clutched the other, and the two dragged Chapman until all three reached Dutch soil.

—

At the clinic, Edith went about her undercover business as usual. More soldiers arrived. She gave them food and hiding places. She found them routes to Holland. The escaping soldiers were her responsibility and the source of the risks she lived with. Edith wouldn't have had it any other way. She developed a wonderful affection for every one of her soldiers. It was affection with a strong current of tension as Edith could never be sure how close the Germans were to exposing the clinic's dangerous secrets.

Chapter Nine

WORRY

As 1915 moved into springtime, Edith was worried. She talked to no one about her anxiety – not to her nurses nor to the people she worked with in the secret network. Her attitude remained positive, and the expression on her face was as serene as ever. But she knew she had to be on constant guard. The signs of trouble were all around, even inside the clinic.

Edith's first reason for concern arose in late November 1914, when Millicent White was forced to get out of Belgium. White had joined the clinic in 1912 as a senior nurse, becoming one of Edith's favorites. She was in her late twenties, Irish, strong-minded and attractive, with deep brown hair that fell to her waist when she let it down. Like many of Edith's nurses, White worked in outside hospitals during the autumn, when there was a lull in patients arriving for care at the clinic. White's nursing

Edith loved her two dogs, Don (on the right) and Jackie. Jackie outlived his mistress by many years. On his death, he was stuffed, mounted, and put on display in Norwich as the loyal pet of the First World War's great heroine. (The Royal London Hospital Archives)

assignment took her to the Royal Palace, which had been turned into a hospital for wounded German soldiers. Somehow, possibly as a result of her forthright personality, she got on the wrong side of a German officer. He threatened to charge her with a military offense.

"What offense?" she demanded.

"Espionage!" the officer thundered.

White knew the Germans had no evidence of espionage against her. Still, she thought it was time to make herself scarce from Brussels and return to England. Edith agreed that her senior nurse had made an enemy who could take away her freedom. But White was determined not to leave Belgium empty-handed. She knew that Colonel Dudley Boger, who was still in the clinic at the time, had written dispatches containing information useful to the British army. She decided to smuggle them out of the country.

White bandaged the dispatches around her thighs, under her long skirt. Equipped with one of Edith's supply of fake passports, White traveled by barge on the canals and rivers from Brussels to the Belgian port city of Antwerp. At a lock on one of the canals, German officials boarded the barge to search the passengers. When the Germans reached White, they were entranced by her luxurious hair. Nothing else interested them, certainly not the possibility of dispatches bandaged to her legs. After they were finally done with the close examination of her hair, they allowed White to continue her trip on the barge.

Four days later, Millicent White reached England by ship and delivered Colonel Boger's dispatches to the British War Office. She was proud to say that the German officer at the Royal Palace was now right: She had committed an act close to espionage against the enemy.

—

The loss of Millicent White was far from the only problem that Edith dealt with in the clinic's operations. Marie, the German maid, presented concerns from the time Edith took up her secret work. Marie was well

aware of what was going on, and though Edith appreciated the maid's efficiency and hard work, she wondered about Marie's loyalties. *Could Marie
be acting as an informant to the Germans in Brussels, revealing secrets that
could bring the deepest trouble to the clinic?* Edith wasn't sure, and every
day, doubts about Marie filled her with apprehension.

"Marie has been giving me a good deal of trouble," Edith wrote in a
letter to her mother, dated March 14, 1915. It was taken to Mrs. Cavell by
one of the escaping British soldiers. "I expect I shall have to send her
away one of these days," Edith wrote, "but must wait in prudence, till
after the war."

Assuming that Marie was untrustworthy, Edith's dilemma was that the
maid would go straight to the Germans with every piece of information
the minute Edith dismissed her from the clinic. But if Edith did nothing
about Marie, the maid would have the chance to pile up even more
damning evidence against Edith. Either way, the secret network could
come to grief.

Edith delayed making a decision about her maid for months. She kept
Marie on the job through the spring and into July, when she finally told
Marie to pack her bags and leave. Nobody ever established whether the
mysterious Marie was or wasn't a German spy. She left behind nothing
that answered the question of her allegiance. In the end, Marie's status
probably made no difference to Edith's state of mind; a spy or not a spy,
Marie brought anxiety to her employer for all the time of Edith's work
with the escaping soldiers.

—

Through the spring, the Germans seemed to be everywhere in the clinic's
neighborhood. In March, German officials set up a minor command post
across the street from one of the four houses that made up the clinic. The
location was probably just a coincidence and had no implications for Edith
and the secret network. Still, the command post made her unsettled.

At the same time, a group of German soldiers took over a house on Rue de la Culture as their own personal barracks. At night, everyone in the top stories of the clinic could see the soldiers in their rooms, drinking and playing cards.

Edith didn't think of the soldiers as a threat, but their presence on the street meant that the British at the clinic needed to be especially alert in not drawing the Germans' attention. The slightest slip could bring the enemy to the door of anyone with even a mild connection to the Allied cause.

———

Louise Thuliez arrived at the clinic, escorting two British soldiers, in early April 1915. Thuliez was the schoolteacher from the village near Bellignies who had begun her secret work by leading British soldiers to the de Croys' château. Her activities grew to include trips into Brussels, where she put soldiers in Edith's care. On the journeys, Thuliez passed herself off as a Salvation Army officer, a disguise that the Germans always fell for. She visited the clinic so often that she became familiar with all the details of Edith's operations. Still, on the trip in early April, Thuliez was surprised at how many British soldiers were hiding in the clinic. She counted thirty-five of them in the four houses – a high number to keep from the Germans' notice indefinitely.

It wasn't just the steady stream of British escapees that made the clinic such a busy place in the spring months. Edith and her nurses were also caring for Belgian patients, who filled the beds in most wards. The Germans were no longer sending their wounded soldiers to the clinic; instead, they shipped the men back home for treatment. Now it was Belgian patients, suffering from illnesses or injuries, that kept Edith and her nurses occupied day and night.

The new clinic on Rue Brussels was another responsibility for Edith. In the early months of the war, construction of the clinic had come to a halt. Building materials were stuck on trains that no longer operated, and men in the construction trades were swept into the Belgian army. But in the spring, work resumed, and Edith became hopeful that the building would soon be ready.

"The new clinic is advancing and becoming habitable," Edith wrote in the March 11 letter to her mother, "but it will not be finished for May 1 when we should be installed."

Edith was overly optimistic when she suggested the clinic was close to being finished. As things turned out, the new place wouldn't be up and running until the fall of 1915. Still, Edith's dream of working there filled her with excitement for many months.

—

In all her duties at the clinic, Edith worked without the guidance of the founder and chief surgeon, Antoine Depage. Early in the war, the doctor joined the Belgian army, taking his medical skills into the fight against the Germans. He stayed with the army when it was driven into France, and Edith accepted the realization that if she was ever to see the doctor again, it would be only when the war ended.

Dr. Depage's wife, Marie, was also gone from Brussels. She sailed to the United States in early 1915 to ask Belgian Americans for donations to help finance the new clinic. On her return trip at the beginning of May, Madame Depage left from New York for England on a majestic British liner named the *Lusitania*, which was carrying almost two thousand crew and passengers. As the *Lusitania* passed the southern tip of Ireland on May 7, a German submarine fired a single torpedo at the ship. The *Lusitania* sank in eighteen minutes, taking 1,198 passengers and crew to their deaths. In all, 761 men, women, and children survived. Marie Depage wasn't one of them.

—

The clinic was packed with men waiting to set off for the Dutch border, and the British soldiers grew restless when the wait lasted more than three or four days. The soldiers were young, full of energy, and frustrated at being stuck in the clinic's crowded cellars and attics. To give the men a chance to blow off a little steam, Edith allowed them out on strolls after dark. But she warned the soldiers to stick to the back streets, not to talk English, and to walk alone or in silent pairs. They were to make themselves as inconspicuous as possible.

Before long, the soldiers were ignoring Edith's rules. They got into the habit of stopping at neighborhood bars for a few beers. The local Belgian drinkers welcomed them. None of the British dreamed they were taking risks since German soldiers drank in different bars. But, one night, things turned dangerous. Edith was away from the clinic, staying with friends in another part of Brussels, on the night that six or seven Irish soldiers knocked back too many beers. When they stepped out of the bar and into the street at the end of the evening, they ambled down Rue de la Culture singing "It's a long way to Tipperary" – a popular Allied wartime song – at the top of their lungs.

Miraculously, no Germans rushed out at the sound of the loud Irish voices. Nobody appeared from the command post or from the boarding-house for German soldiers. Apparently they slept through the whole noisy episode. But a doctor at the clinic awoke. Alarmed at the racket, he rounded up the singing Irishmen and locked them in a ward.

Edith arrived back at the clinic before seven the next morning. If she was annoyed by the Irish soldiers' musical night, or frightened about what it might lead to, she kept her calm manner. Her concern was to get the Irish out of the clinic. She contacted members of her group, who agreed to take in the soldiers. In the quiet of the early morning, the Irish were hurried through the streets to their new quarters. Edith braced herself for a visit from German officials, asking questions about the singing. But no Germans appeared. Edith hoped she had survived another crisis.

—

When Charlie Scott came to Edith in early April, he was running a high fever and felt so weak that he could hardly stand. Scott was the young soldier from the Norfolk Regiment who had been hidden for eight months by the miner Désiré Richez at his cottage in Wiheries. During this long time, the wounds to Scott's chest had grown worse. He needed expert medical care, something Richez hadn't a hope of providing. Besides the worry about Scott's health, Richez was nervous that the Germans had targeted his cottage. It was probably a matter of days before they would discover Scott's hiding place in a hole inside the kitchen wall. Richez acted quickly, and with the help of other members of the secret network, he smuggled Scott to Brussels and to Edith.

She put Scott into a bed and dressed his wounds. Since Edith and Scott were a couple of Norfolk natives, they shared happy stories of their home county. Scott felt relieved and protected. But his sense of comfort ended late the next night, when Edith shook him awake. "I am in trouble," she said. "You will have to come with me."

Edith helped the young soldier down the stairs and across the yard behind the clinic to a shed, which held large barrels of green apples. Edith cleared one barrel of enough apples to make room for Scott to fit inside. Then she covered him in apples, spreading them loosely so that he had enough air to breathe. Scott squatted down and listened for sounds in the silent night.

Soon, he could make out the thump of boots on the stairs inside the clinic. He knew that German soldiers had arrived, though he was never told how Edith learned in advance that they planned a raid on Rue de la Culture that night. The boots came closer, into the backyard. Scott heard German voices. He held himself rigid, not daring to move, as he listened to the soldiers poke around the yard. But nobody disturbed his barrel, and after a while, the Germans strode back into the clinic. Several more minutes of Scott's excruciating wait went by before silence fell once again. The Germans had left the building.

Edith pulled Scott out of the barrel, and in the next days, she hired guides to take him to Holland. Charlie Scott was home in England before the middle of April, another soldier saved by Edith's ingenuity and nerve.

—

For some British soldiers, escape from the Germans was an adventure full of excitement. For others, it was a necessary part of their jobs as soldiers, one they would have preferred to avoid. Since they had no choice, they made the best of the situation. For a few soldiers, the challenge of avoiding the clutches of the Germans became a terrible strain that affected their health for the worse. Ernest Stanton of the 4th Battalion, Middlesex Regiment was one of the men whose health suffered from the stress.

When Stanton was left behind after the fighting at Mons, Auguste Joly and his wife, Sidonie, hid him in the small cottage where they lived in Wiheries. Joly was the miner known in the secret organization mainly as a guide who led the escaping soldiers to Brussels. But Auguste and Sidonie took one soldier into their home, and he was Ernest Stanton. The Jolys kept him in the little cottage for seven months, a time of almost unbearable tension for Stanton.

He was a large man, over six feet tall, with a husky build. His size made him an awkward fit for the tiny room where he spent most of his time. Even tinier was the place where Stanton hid when the Germans made one of their frequent inspections. At each German raid, Stanton squeezed into an empty cistern, under the cottage's floor. The cistern was the size of an ordinary barrel, barely wide enough to hold him. As soon as he slid into the cistern, Auguste Joly popped a lid on top, and Stanton sweated out the wait until the Germans left the cottage.

By the time Stanton was led to Edith's clinic in April, he had become a nervous wreck. He felt worn down, as if he couldn't go on for another day, and one morning, he made the frightening discovery that he was unable to speak. The worry and trouble of the past seven months had caused the power of speech to desert poor Stanton.

Edith took special care of the soldier. She spent as much time as she could with him, trying to ease his anxieties. By the time he left the clinic, guided on his way back to England, his speech had finally returned.

At home, Stanton's general health improved. He married his sweetheart and settled down after the war. But the strange loss of speech returned to Stanton one more time. As in Belgium, it was temporary, and he was soon able to speak again. The loss lasted for just one day. It was the day of Edith's funeral.

—

Edith did her best to conceal the strain that the secret work put her under. It wasn't her nature to complain or express regret. If it was too much for Edith to deal every day with raiding Germans, with Irish soldiers who made too much noise in the night, with a maid who might be a spy, with the potential dangers to her own nurses, with the hundreds of British soldiers coming to her for help, and with all of the burdens that were heaped on her, nobody heard a word of protest. She was strong, and she had been given a duty to carry out.

Still, during the winter and spring of 1915, Edith showed small signs that she was aware of the far less stressful life she once led and might yet be leading if her fate had been different. On March 11, she wrote a letter to Eddy Cavell, the man she had once thought she would marry. The letter, which reached Eddy through an escaped British soldier, told him some of the details that were safe to reveal about her activities in Brussels. She hoped Eddy was well and wondered if he was still managing the small farm. Then she ended the letter with a longing for the way she lived years earlier. "I like to look back on the days when we were young," Edith wrote to Eddy, "and life was fresh and beautiful and the country so desirable and sweet."

Chapter Ten

THE GERMANS CLOSE IN

P hilippe Baucq was probably the first member of the secret organization to warn Edith about the German threat to her and the clinic. Baucq was a latecomer to the organization, joining it in February 1915, but once in, he became an aggressive operator. By profession, he was an architect. He was in his midthirties and lived in the Brussels suburb of Schaerbeck with his wife and two daughters. As a young man, he swam for Belgium in international competitions, and as an adult, he still kept fit. He was a man who had lots of energy and, as he later revealed, a taste for drama.

Baucq began his anti-German work by distributing copies of *La Libre Belgique*, an underground newspaper that carried reports about the war in defiance of the German ban on a free Belgian press. The paper printed twenty-five thousand copies per issue and published five issues each

Philippe Baucq was a Brussels architect who served valiantly in the secret organization that aided escaping British, French, and Belgian soldiers. The Germans punished him for his brave defiance by sentencing him to the same fate as Edith. (The Royal London Hospital Archives)

month. For the entire war, *La Libre Belgique* kept to its schedule, which drove the Germans mad with frustration.

Even though Baucq had plenty to handle in his distribution work, he threw himself into every level of the secret organization's activity. First, he arranged for places where escaping soldiers could hide in Brussels. Then he connected with the guides. Finally, he became a guide himself, escorting the soldiers through occupied territory to the border. It was as if Baucq wanted to test his courage against the greatest possible dangers.

He developed contacts with politicians in Brussels. They were people who didn't necessarily support the German occupiers, but knew everything that the Germans were up to. From one source, Baucq learned in late April that the Germans had assigned a new agency to arrest everyone who aided Allied soldiers in escaping from Belgium. The agency, called Section B of the German political police, was under the direction of two fanatical officers – Lieutenant Ernest Bergan and Sergeant Henri Pinkhoff. Though the two were committed to bringing down the entire escape organization, they took particular aim at Edith. They suspected that she was at the core of the organization, and each day, Bergan and Pinkhoff repeated a mantra to one another: "The Cavell woman must go before a firing squad."

Philippe Baucq reported what he learned to Edith. It was the first and only time that the two met privately, and at the meeting, Edith gave Baucq the impression that she wasn't surprised by his news. She told him that strange things were happening at the clinic. Men she described as "suspicious persons" called on her for help in leaving Belgium. They wanted money, rooms to hide in, and guides to take them to the border. Edith

OPPOSITE: La Libre Belgique *was an underground newspaper published by Belgian patriots throughout the war, bringing news to their fellow citizens in defiance of the German ban. The clandestine paper survived Governor-General von Bissing's "reward for the discovery of its office and made fun of him by faking a picture of him reading their condemned paper."* (The Royal London Hospital Archives)

NUMÉRO 30   JUIN 1915

PRIX DU NUMÉRO — élastique, de zéro à l'infini (prière aux revendeurs de ne pas dépasser cette limite)

LA LIBRE BELGIQUE

Acceptons provisoirement les sacrifices qui nous sont imposés....... et attendons patiemment l'heure de la réparation.
Le Bourgmestre
ADOLPHE MAX.

FONDÉE
LE 1er FÉVRIER 1915

Envers ces personnes qui dominent par la force militaire notre pays, ayons les égards que commande l'intérêt général. Respectons les règlements qu'elles nous imposent aussi longtemps qu'ils ne portent atteinte ni à la liberté de nos consciences chrétienne ni à notre *Dignité Patriotique.*
Mgr MERCIER.

BULLETIN DE PROPAGANDE PATRIOTIQUE — RÉGULIÈREMENT IRRÉGULIER
NE SE SOUMETTANT A AUCUNE CENSURE

| ADRESSE TÉLÉGRAPHIQUE ·
 KOMMANDANTUR - BRUXELLES | BUREAUX ET ADMINISTRATION <br> ne pouvant être un emplacement de tout repos, ils sont installés dans une cave automobile | ANNONCES : Les affaires étant nulles sous la domination allemande, nous avons supprimé la page d'annonces et conseillons à nos clients de réserver leur argent pour des temps meilleurs. |

AVIS.

On nous fait à nouveau l'honneur de s'occuper de notre modeste bulletin. Nous en sommes flattés, mais nous nous voyons forcés de répéter ce que nous avons déjà dit pour notre défense. Ce n'est certes pas nous qu'on peut accuser sans manquer à la vérité, de provoquer nos concitoyens à la révolte. Nous ne manquons pas une occasion de prêcher la patience, l'endurance, le calme et le respect des lois de la guerre. Aussi profitons-nous de cette occasion qui nous est offerte pour répéter l'avis que nous avons déjà inséré :

RESTONS CALMES !!!

Le jour viendra (lentement mais surement) où nos ennemis contraints de reculer devant les Alliés, devront abandonner notre capitale.

Souvenons-nous alors des avis nombreux qui ont été donnés aux civils par le Gouvernement et par notre bourgmestre.

SON EXCELLENCE LE GOUVERNEUR Bon VON BISSING ET SON AMIE INTIME

NOTRE CHER GOUVERNEUR, ÉCŒURÉ PAR LA LECTURE DES MENSONGES DES JOURNAUX CENSURÉS, CHERCHE LA VÉRITÉ DANS LA « LIBRE BELGIQUE »

M. Max : SOYONS CALMES!!!

Faisons taire les sentiments de légitime colère qui fermentent en nos cœurs.

Soyons, comme nous l'avons été jusqu'ici, respectueux des lois de la guerre. C'est ainsi que nous continuerons à mériter l'estime et l'admiration de tous les peuples civilisés.

Ce serait une INUTILE LA-CHETÉ, *une lâcheté indigne des Belges que de chercher à se venger ailleurs que sur le champ de bataille. Ce serait de plus* EX-POSER DES INNOCENTS *à des représailles terribles de la part d'ennemis sans pitié et sans justice.*

Méfions-nous des agents provocateurs allemands qui, en exaltant notre patriotisme, nous pousseraient à commettre des excès.

RESTONS MAITRES DE NOUS-MÊMES ET PRÊCHONS LE CALME AUTOUR DE NOUS. C'EST LE PLUS GRAND SERVICE QUE NOUS PUISSIONS RENDRE A NOTRE CHÈRE PATRIE.

L'ORDRE SOCIAL TOUT ENTIER DÉFENDU PAR LA BELGIQUE.

Le 3 août, le Gouvernement allemand remet à la Belgique une note demandant le libre passage pour ses armées sur son territoire, moyennant quoi l'Allemagne s'engage à maintenir l'intégrité du royaume et de ses possessions. Sinon, la Belgique sera traitée en ennemie. Le roi Albert a douze heures pour répondre. Devant cet ultimatum, il n'hésite pas. Il sait que l'armée allemande est une force terrible. Il connaît l'empe-reur allemand. Il sait que l'orgueilleux, après une telle démarche, ne reculera plus. Son trône est en jeu, plus que son trône . les sept millions d'âmes — quelle éloquence prennent les vulgaires termes des statistiques dans certaines circonstances ! — qui lui sont confiées . il voit en esprit ce beau pays indéfendable : ces charbonnages, ces carrières, ces usines, ces filatures, ces ports, cette florissante industrie épanouie dans ces plaines ouvertes qu'il ne pourra pas préserver. Mais il s'agit d'un traité où il y a sa signature. Répondre oui à l'Allemagne, c'est trahir ses consignataires, le

PRIÈRE DE FAIRE CIRCULER CE BULLETIN

sensed that the men weren't genuine escapees, and she pretended not to know what they were talking about. Edith presented herself to them as just a nurse who looked after the sick and injured.

Baucq cautioned Edith to take care. She assured him that she was keeping her wits about her. But the organization's work was essential, and she intended to carry on with it as long as could.

—

Within two weeks of the meeting with Baucq, Edith sent an urgent message to Jeanne de Belleville, the countess who lived near Bellignies. Like Louise Thuliez, the countess had become a guide escorting British and French soldiers from the Bellignies area to Brussels. Both women survived desperate adventures. On one trip, Thuliez was in charge of a British soldier who thought she might not be a real member of the escape network. He kept his pistol loaded and ready for firing; if Thuliez made a false step, he intended to shoot her. When Thuliez steered the soldier safely to his destination, he realized he had been mistaken. The soldier apologized. Thuliez shrugged, as if to say that the chance of being shot by someone on her own side was just one of the hazards of war.

Edith respected both Thuliez and de Belleville as her courageous colleagues, but, in mid-May, in Edith's urgent message to de Belleville, she begged the countess and others at the Bellignies end of the network not to bring men to the clinic in the next week. "My situation," Edith wrote, "is becoming more and more strained every day."

British soldiers had been coming to the clinic in steady numbers, and even though they were now staying only a day or two before Edith moved them on their way to the border, the increased chance of drawing German surveillance alarmed her. Edith had taken Philippe Baucq's warning to heart, and, for a short time, she scaled back the clinic's escape operations.

—

But soon enough, by late May, the arrival of soldiers in the usual numbers started up again. Edith couldn't bear the thought of turning away her fellow countrymen. She was delighted when a lance corporal named Horace Sheldrake reached the clinic. At thirty-seven, Sheldrake was older than the other soldiers. Edith appreciated his maturity, but best of all, he was another Norfolk native. Though their meeting was brief, the two felt much warmth for one another, two people from the same rural English county caught in the horror of war. Edith gave Sheldrake money, a pipe, tobacco, and a comfortable hospital shirt. The gifts were intended to cheer him on his trip to the border.

To Sheldrake's dismay, the Germans caught him as he left Brussels. He spent the next years as a prisoner of war. When Sheldrake arrived home at the war's end, he still had the hospital shirt. He told his family how much he admired Edith, and he insisted that, on his death, he be buried in the shirt she gave him. When Sheldrake died in 1946, his family carried out the wish.

—

A few days after Sheldrake passed through the clinic, Edith had a warm encounter with yet another Norfolk soldier. He was Robert William Mapes of the 1st Norfolk Regiment, a private who had been wounded at Mons by a German bullet that drilled through his ankle. He recuperated while he hid for several months with a family in the nearby village of Quiévrain. When Jeanne de Belleville heard about Mapes, she organized the fake passport and the system of guides that led him to a large house in Brussels. Many English soldiers were staying at the house, and while Mapes was there, waiting to move on to Holland, he met Edith.

Mapes never knew who owned the house where he was sheltered, but the owner was part of the secret organization and a colleague of Edith's. She visited the house one day and immediately recognized, from Mapes' accent, that he was a Norfolk native. The two began a conversation, and

Edith soon learned that Mapes came from Hethersett, a village not far from Swardeston. Nostalgia overcame her.

"Dear old Norfolk," she said to Mapes. "I would do anything to help a Norfolkman."

Edith put her arms around Mapes and gave him a kiss, something that she did not do often. But, at that moment, with the Germans closing in on her, she must have felt homesick for the part of England she shared with the soldier she held in her arms. He was on his way back home. Edith may have sensed that it could be a long time before she saw Norfolk again.

—

Raoul de Roy was a young Belgian who lived south of Brussels. He wanted more than anything to get to England, where he could join the army and fight against the Germans. Jeanne de Belleville had known de Roy since he was a little boy, and she promised to make his wish come true. Early in May 1915, she gave de Roy a fake passport and took him by train to Brussels.

As a precaution, since the countess had been active in the secret organization for so long and was aware that the Germans might have taken note of her activities, she and de Roy sat in different sections of the train. When they reached the station in Brussels, she wrote the address of Edith's clinic on notepaper and slipped it to de Roy, whispering to him that he must memorize the address, then rip up the notepaper. De Roy not only ripped the paper into pieces, he also swallowed them.

He made his way to the clinic and explained his mission to Edith. She nodded and gave de Roy a form to sign. The form was for an operation. De Roy was puzzled.

"But, Madame," he said to Edith, "I don't need an operation. I want you to get me across the border."

Edith gave de Roy a smile. "That, young man," she said, "is the operation!"

Edith was only partly joking. While it was true that the clinic had no intention of performing an operation on de Roy, with many of the escaping men, Edith put their names into the book where she kept her official list of real medical operations. Then, opposite the names, she wrote imaginary treatments that the men received for fictitious ailments and illnesses. If the Germans happened to ask Edith why certain men had stayed at the clinic, she could produce the book as explanation. No record exists today that reveals whether Edith ever used the operations book to get herself out of tight spots, but it was typical of her careful and methodical planning that she prepared herself for every possible trouble.

Young Raoul de Roy stayed at the clinic for three days before leaving with a party of three or four other men for the trip into Holland. At the border, they ran into a problem. Strands of barbed wire guarded that section of the frontier, and beneath the barbed wire, hand grenades were buried in the sand. De Roy and the others solved the difficulty by stepping on the least thick barbed wire and performing a balancing act to keep from falling on the grenades. De Roy reached England, where he joined the 7th Artillery Regiment. Just as he had dreamed, he fought the Germans for the rest of the war.

Like all of the soldiers who passed through the clinic, de Roy never forgot his debt to Edith. During his three days on Rue de la Culture, he talked with her several times and formed a lasting impression of Edith. To de Roy, she was an easy person to get on with. But she was more than that; she had "spontaneity." Even in the period of her growing worry, Edith was generous to the men who were under her care.

—

On June 14, a man named Otto Mayer came to Edith's office at number 149. His appearance in the clinic represented the worst nightmare Edith could have imagined. Mayer worked for Bergan and Pinkhoff of the German political police. Although he was a German civilian, not an army man, Mayer had assets that made him valuable to Bergan and Pinkhoff. Unlike them, he spoke English as well as German and French. Like them, he was expert at double-dealing, a skilled sneak who would be effective on the Cavell case.

On the June day when Mayer showed up at Edith's office, she was over on Rue Brussels, checking on the construction of the new clinic. It's possible that Mayer chose this time when Edith was absent for his surprise visit, hoping that the less experienced nurses would crumble under his questioning. Elisabeth Wilkins, an Englishwoman in her late twenties, was sitting at Edith's desk the moment Mayer walked in. It was lucky for Edith that, of all the nurses, Wilkins was the one on duty. She had senior status, and she was more assured under pressure than the others.

"May I do something for you?" she asked Mayer.

He answered with a brusque question. "Have you got any more?"

Wilkins thought the man must be referring to nurses. The clinic had received several requests for nursing staff, and Mayer, who was dressed in civilian clothes, seemed to be on the same errand.

"I'm sorry," she said, "we have no nurses available."

"I'm not talking about nurses," Mayer snapped, turning around the lapel on his jacket to reveal the badge of the German political police. "Have you any more British soldiers in the clinic?"

Wilkins kept her composure. She knew that two British soldiers had left the clinic just the day before, and that no more British were there at the moment. But on the floor above her, two French and two Belgian soldiers were waiting in a ward to leave for Holland. In the desk where Wilkins was sitting, her Matron's desk, Edith kept names and records of the soldiers who had passed through the clinic. These weren't just lists of operations performed, but detailed accounts of British escapees. At all costs, Wilkins had to get Mayer out of number 149.

"We have no British soldiers here," she said. "If you don't believe me, come over to my room. You can go through my desk and look anywhere else in the house you want."

Mayer followed Wilkins to number 145, where he made a search of her desk. Then he questioned the patients in the ward. Wilkins knew Mayer would find nothing; her desk held no incriminating records, and the men in the beds were Belgian civilians. While Mayer searched and interrogated, Wilkins slipped back to 149. She sent the two French and two Belgian soldiers to safe houses in the neighborhood, then she hid Edith's records in a toilet tank.

After Mayer finished with Wilkins' building, he demanded to look through everything in Edith's office and in the ward above. Wilkins told him to go ahead. Mayer wouldn't come across anything damaging – unless he was such a meticulous detective that he examined the toilet tank. Wilkins took a deep breath and watched in relief as Mayer walked past the toilet. He was a disappointed man when he left the clinic. And he warned Wilkins that he would be back.

—

That night in her office, Edith wrote the last letter to her mother that ever reached Mrs. Cavell. Edith chose her words carefully. She wrote about everyday events, about the little garden at the new clinic, about the hot weather and severe thunderstorms in Brussels. But, in the course of the letter, she included remarks that tried to warn her mother of Edith's fears for the future. She wrote of "very serious" things happening, the "very" underlined, and she emphasized that "I am not sure of having another occasion of sending [letters]."

Otto Mayer's search of the clinic had shaken Edith more than anything the Germans had so far done, and she was trying to let Mrs. Cavell know that Edith believed she could be arrested at any moment. She had endured searches in the past by regular German army officers, but Mayer represented a threat on a far more serious level. Mayer and the others in the German political police were certain to be more purposeful: It was their job to keep after the secret network until they caught all of its members. Edith was pessimistic about what lay ahead, and she needed to prepare her mother for the bad news that was sure to come.

—

In the next few days, Edith was distracted – something that was out of the ordinary for such a self-contained person. A Belgian surgeon whom she assisted in an operation told Edith that she was "jumpy." She developed the habit of peeking around the curtains in the front windows of the clinic, examining the street for signs of German activity. Edith was on edge.

And then another search team from the German political police arrived at the clinic. Edith was in a second-floor ward. Once again she heard the sound of German boots pounding up the stairs. In an instant, she threw the documents she was holding into a fireplace and put a match to them. Earlier that month, right after Mayer's visit, Edith had burned several of her papers listing the names and details of British soldiers. But she still kept many more documents in different places around the clinic. It may seem puzzling that Edith saved records that were guaranteed to get her in trouble with the Germans. But to her, it made sense to keep the paper-work. When the war was over, she would be required to account for every part of the clinic's operation to her boss, Antoine Depage. The material about the British soldiers was part of the record, and to destroy the documents offended her sense of responsibility. She would almost rather be imprisoned than fail in her duty to Dr. Depage.

—

Soon Princess Marie de Croy traveled from Bellignies to the clinic for a discussion about the secret organization's work. The visit took place just one day after the latest German raid, and Edith, who wasn't expecting the princess, was shocked to find her waiting in the office.

"I wish you hadn't come," she said. "I am evidently suspect."

She led Princess Marie to the office window overlooking the street in front of the clinic. Edith pointed to a group of men who were standing around a spot in the pavement that apparently needed repairs.

"Those men have been outside for days," she said. "They hardly work at all. I'm certain they've been sent to watch me."

The princess told Edith that the reason for her visit was to call an end to the network's activities. She said the Germans appeared to have almost everyone under surveillance. Bellignies had been raided several times. Now was the time to stop.

Edith agreed, but she had a question. "Are there any more hidden men?"

"About thirty," the princess answered. Louise Thuliez had found the thirty soldiers hiding near a village named Cambrai.

"Then we can't stop just yet," Edith said. "If one of those men were taken and shot, it would be our fault."

The two women came to an understanding. They would carry on until the last thirty soldiers were out of Belgium. But they wouldn't take the thirty by way of Bellignies or the clinic. With the Germans watching both places, that would be foolish. By the time the princess left Edith's office, both knew that the secret network was still in business, at least for another month.

—

Edith changed her mind about not taking more British soldiers into the clinic. In July, she accepted six or seven of them. In her opinion, this was unavoidable because the soldiers had nowhere else to go. She hid them in the cellar, gave them whatever they needed to get to the Dutch border, and provided money and guides.

Two of the soldiers, Matty Shiells and Pat Revelly, were from the Royal Irish Rifles, and for them, Edith thought up a clever disguise. She dressed them as monks from a religious order whose members wore white robes and observed a vow of silence. Edith and the soldiers found the outfits amusing, but the laughs ended when the three sat down in the streetcar that was taking them to the outskirts of Brussels. Edith noticed that a German officer across the aisle was staring at Revelly's feet. *What was so fascinating?* Then Edith caught on. When Revelly's white robe was hiked up, the German could see that Revelly was wearing British army boots. She hurried the two soldiers off the streetcar and pointed them on their route north to Holland. Within a few weeks, Shiells and Revelly rejoined the Royal Irish Rifles.

—

Helping the two Irishmen successfully was probably Edith's last piece of work for the secret organization. Time was running out. Through July, the German political police conducted more searches at the clinic, and a Frenchman named George Gaston Quien, who worked as a German secret agent, infiltrated both the clinic and the Mons-Bellignies part of the organization. Quien claimed to be a French army officer who fought at Charleroi. His story might have been believable since he had a damaged foot, which he claimed he suffered in battle. That wasn't true; the injury resulted from a civilian accident. Nevertheless, Edith's clinic gave him medical treatment, and Quien, who could be charming, took advantage of his stay in one of the wards to flirt with the nurses in hopes of getting information about the secret organization. Edith thought Quien was a phony from the start, but he still managed to gather several damaging facts before he left.

Edith sensed trouble all around her. She had documents that she was determined to save, and unknown to anyone else until much later, she hid the papers under a loose floorboard in a bar called *Chez Jules*, down the street from the clinic. Edith expected one day to retrieve the hidden documents.

—

Philippe Baucq was the first member of the network arrested by the German political police. Sergeant Henri Pinkhoff and six of his plain-clothes officers showed up at Baucq's house at 10:30 on Saturday night, July 31. It happened to be a night when Louise Thuliez, in Brussels to arrange for a group of Belgians to escape to Holland, was staying at the Baucq home. Pinkhoff knew all about Thuliez. He placed her under arrest along with Baucq.

Pinkhoff, a short-tempered man, came close to arresting Baucq's thirteen-year-old daughter, Yvonne, who was upstairs in the house. Hearing the German police on the ground floor and knowing that her father had just received four thousand copies of *La Libre Belgique* for distribution, Yvonne was frantic to ensure that the Germans didn't find the newspapers. She began to throw them out of a second-story window. Some of the papers were still in tied bundles. One bundle, plummeting from the window, hit a police officer on the head. The Germans rushed up the stairs and grabbed Yvonne. It was only her young age that kept Pinkhoff from arresting her.

When the Germans left the house, they took Baucq and Thuliez to Section B's offices, then to St. Gilles Prison, where the two would soon be joined in captivity by other members of the secret network.

—

In the next five days, in raids in Brussels, Mons, Bellignies, and other towns and villages on both sides of the French border, the Germans swept up virtually everyone in the network. Among those arrested were Princess Marie de Croy and Countess Jeanne de Belleville; the two miners, Auguste Joly and Désiré Richez; and the two pharmacists, Georges Derveau and Louis Séverin. They led away the men from Mons: Herman Capiau, the engineer, and Albert Libiez, the lawyer. Section B had good information on the network, and they caught guides, couriers, and even the spouses of network members. Before they finished, Pinkhoff and his men carried off a total of thirty-five people to prison.

One person the Germans didn't catch was Princess Marie's brother, Prince Reginald de Croy. When the prince heard about Baucq's arrest, he hurried from Bellignies to Brussels to warn other members of the organization that they must go into hiding. Edith told him she hadn't a chance of escaping the Germans. She chose to wait and meet her fate. Edith was certain that imprisonment would come soon.

Prince Reginald went from the clinic to Ada Bodart's house. She was the Irishwoman who sheltered many escaping soldiers. Bodart had recently been widowed and lived alone with her teenage son, Philippe. She thanked the prince for the warning. When Prince Reginald told Bodart that he was headed for another network member's home to spread the word to him, she volunteered to do the errand, taking Philippe with her. They reached the network member's house, but Pinkhoff and his men were already there. They took Bodart and Philippe to prison. Prince Reginald escaped and remained free for the entire war.

—

Edith was one of the last members of the network arrested by the Germans. Henri Pinkhoff, Otto Mayer, and a small squad of soldiers drove to the clinic on the afternoon of August 5. It was a moment that Pinkhoff relished, putting an end to the career of the infuriating woman who smuggled so many British and French soldiers back to their own countries. He made the most of the occasion, stomping around Edith's office, throwing her papers on the floor, shouting at Edith and her nurses. His performance lasted almost two hours, and when Pinkhoff was done, he placed Edith under arrest. He arrested Elisabeth Wilkins too, though she was soon released. There would be no release for Edith. When Pinkhoff and his men drove her away in the German army car, Edith's freedom had come to an end.

Chapter Eleven

THE TRIAL

The Germans locked Edith in cell number 23 at St. Gilles Prison. St. Gilles was vast, ancient, and frightening; Philippe Baucq wrote that "it gives one the cold and sad impression that one feels before a funeral monument." Cell 23, 4 meters by 2½ meters, had a sink, a small open cupboard, a metal bucket, one chair, and a folding bed, which was converted into a table during the day by closing it and laying boards across the top. Edith ate her prison meals at the table: coffee and bread for breakfast; potatoes, grilled meat, and a glass of weak beer for the main meal at noon; coffee, bread, and cheese for supper. On Sunday evenings, she was allowed a special dinner cooked at the clinic and delivered to St. Gilles by the nurses.

Edith passed the hours in her cell embroidering, reading, and worrying. Her most treasured book, *The Imitation of Christ*, brought her relief. Over

When the Germans arrested Edith in August 1915, they locked her in Brussels' dark and forbidding St. Gilles Prison. Edith remained in St. Gilles for over two months. (The Royal London Hospital Archives)

and over, she read her copy, making notes in the margins and underlining passages that enlightened her. One sentence she marked seemed to speak directly to the ordeal she faced with the Germans: "It is no small prudence to keep silent in an evil time, and inwardly to turn thyself to Me, and not to be troubled by the judgment of men."

Edith's worries weren't about herself, but about those on the outside who depended on her. She was concerned for Grace Jemmett, for her dog, Jackie, and for the young nurses in training at the clinic. She wrote to Elisabeth Wilkins, telling her to make sure the nurses studied hard for their October exams and to ask that a clinic doctor named Heger continue Jemmett's morphine treatment. As for the dog, Edith wrote in another letter, "If Jackie is sad, tell him I will soon be back."

Twice, Wilkins got permission to visit Edith in her cell. The trouble was, Otto Mayer sat in the cell during both visits. Mayer said he was assigned to make sure Wilkins didn't give Edith a capsule of poison to commit suicide. Edith was disgusted that anyone thought she was capable of something as contrary to her beliefs as suicide.

Wilkins delivered one piece of welcome news: The clinic had moved into its new building. Wilkins supervised the transportation of furniture and equipment from Rue de la Culture to Rue Brussels. It was all done by handcart and took several days to complete. Edith was happy about the opening of the new clinic, but saddened not to be a part of the life and work in the building she had done so much to plan.

To brighten the hours in prison, the nurses sent her a bouquet of fresh flowers. Edith wrote to them, encouraging the young women in their work and thanking them for the bouquet.

"Your lovely flowers have made my cell gay," she wrote. "The roses are still fresh, but the chrysanthemums did not like prison any more than I do. Hence, they did not live very long."

—

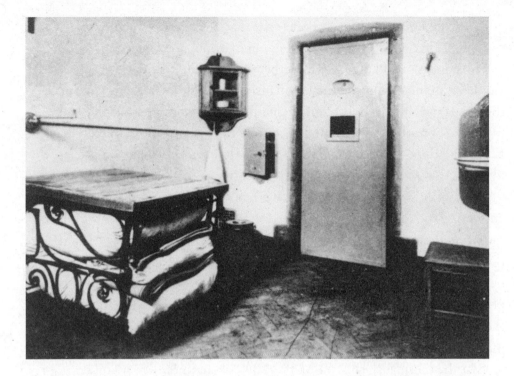

*Edith's cell at St. Gilles Prison was small and spartan, but efficient. The table on
the left turned into a bed at night, when the boards on top were removed and the
mattress and blankets folded out.* (The Royal London Hospital Archives)

For three days during Edith's first weeks in prison – on August 8, 18, and
21 – Lieutenant Bergan and Sergeant Pinkhoff put her through hours of
interrogation in Bergan's prison office. Pinkhoff asked most of the questions, always in French. Since Bergan spoke no French or English,
Pinkhoff repeated the questions and answers to him in German. When
Bergan asked Edith his own questions in German, Pinkhoff again trans-
lated the questions and answers back and forth. Otto Mayer, who spoke
English as well as the other two languages, was present during the questioning, but no English was used during the sessions. A German clerk
named Neuhaus wrote down the proceedings in German. Later, Pinkhoff

edited Neuhaus' record into a document that became Edith's official statement that was submitted to the military tribunal for her trial.

The confusion of languages, together with Pinkhoff's final edit of Edith's statement, allowed the Germans to put their own interpretation on the answers Edith gave. It hardly helped her position that she wasn't permitted to consult a lawyer before or during the interrogation. In fact, Edith had none of the normal rights that Britain gave to a person preparing for a trial proceeding.

None of this discouraged Edith. She had worked out a strategy for answering the questions, no matter what hurdles were put in her way. Her intention was to admit everything, as long as she was reasonably certain that the Germans already knew the answers. She wouldn't lie – that would be unthinkable for Edith, even to an enemy intent on giving her the death penalty – but would tell Bergan and Pinkhoff nothing new. On August 8, the first day of the interrogation, Pinkhoff advised Edith that the other members of the secret organization had confessed to their activities against the Germans. This wasn't true, though all thirty-five members gave statements to the Germans by the time of the trial. Edith had a good idea what the Germans had learned from their sources and from their weeks of surveillance of the clinic. She shaped her answers to Bergan and Pinkhoff to fit her own idea of their knowledge.

Edith admitted that she sheltered British and French soldiers at the clinic and helped them to escape, though she downplayed the numbers. When the German interrogators suggested she had allowed a couple of hundred soldiers to pass through her hands, she agreed, though Edith knew that the final figure was much higher. She admitted that Louise Thuliez, Jeanne de Belleville, and others whom she named brought soldiers to her clinic. And she gave Bergan and Pinkhoff the names of such people as Ada Bodart and Louis Séverin, who hid soldiers in their houses in Brussels. The Germans already knew these details, just as they knew the six locations in the city where escaping soldiers and their guides met before the trips to the Dutch border. Edith felt sure she was revealing to Bergan and Pinkhoff nothing that came as a surprise to them.

In the view of the two German interrogators, Edith made her most damaging admission when she said that many of the English and French soldiers, in fact the majority, were not wounded. They were able-bodied and therefore capable of returning to service in the war against the Germans, after they'd escaped home to Britain and France. Under the German military code, this was one of the most serious offenses. "Conducting soldiers to the enemy," as the offense was called, could get Edith sentenced to death. Bergan and Pinkhoff rubbed their hands in satisfaction over Edith's admission. Now, they thought, they were going to realize their aim of sending Edith Cavell to the firing squad.

———

Late in September, Edith wrote to Elisabeth Wilkins, asking her to come to the prison and bring clothes that Edith listed in the letter: her blue coat and skirt, white muslin blouse, thick reindeer gloves, and her gray fur stole. This was the outfit that Edith planned to wear at the trial. She wasn't yet aware of the trial's date, but she wanted to be ready. Certainly she wouldn't wear her nurse's uniform to court; she put on the uniform only when she was working in the clinic. The clothes she listed in the letter would be appropriate for the courtroom.

It wasn't until Tuesday, October 5, that Edith and the others were informed of the date for their trial. It was just two days away – October 7 – when all thirty-five of the secret network were to be tried as a group by a German military tribunal of five senior officers. Edith felt ready. She was anxious to get on with whatever the Germans had in store for her.

The trial began early on Thursday morning, not in a conventional courtroom, but in a grand setting that the Germans selected as a showcase for staging the important prosecution. The German army wanted all of

Brussels to know that it was dealing severely with anyone who dared to aid the occupying army's enemies. It was in Belgium's Senate chamber that the trial took place, in the same room where King Albert had met with his generals on August 2, 1914, to discuss Germany's ultimatum, which set off the war. The chamber was large, round, plush, and ornate; its color scheme gold and red, its seats covered in velvet. Edith and her colleagues, twenty-two men and thirteen women altogether, sat facing the judges. German army officers, who had come to see what they considered an entertainment that might send people to their deaths, were all around them in the spectator seats.

The man in charge of the prosecution was a tenacious and aggressive counsel named Eduard Stoeber, who was brought in from Bavaria to handle the case. Edith and the other defendants were allowed to retain lawyers, though none of the counsel met with their clients in the days before the trial. It was only on Thursday morning, in the Senate chamber, that Edith was introduced to Sadi Kirschen, a Brussels counsel who was assigned at the last minute to represent her and eight of the other defendants.

—

Stoeber's first witness for the prosecution was Edith. Stoeber called all thirty-five defendants as witnesses, putting them in the strange position of testifying against their own interests. The proceedings, including Stoeber's questions, were in German. A translator repeated the questions in French, and gave Edith's answers, which were in French, to the rest of the court in German. Stoeber's examination of Edith consisted of just twelve questions. Almost all covered the routine of Edith's activities in the secret network, including the names of her associates. But in the next to last question, Stoeber raised the issue that could lead to a death sentence.

"Do you realize," Stoeber asked, "that in [helping men to escape] it would be to the disadvantage of Germany and to the advantage of the enemy?"

The point that Stoeber was getting at was Edith's violation of the section in the German military code against conducting men to the enemy. These were men, in Stoeber's view, who would return to fight against Germany.

"My preoccupation," Edith answered, "has not been to aid the enemy but to help the men who applied to me to reach the frontier. Once across the frontier, they were free."

The defense in Edith's answer was that she concerned herself only with assisting the men to reach Holland. What they did afterwards was beyond her control. The escaped soldiers made their own decisions.

—

At noon, after Stoeber questioned the other defendants, the court recessed for lunch. No food had been arranged for the defendants, who weren't allowed to leave the Senate chamber. But a few of the forty guards on court duty gave them sips of water and samples from the huge tank of soup that was wheeled into the chamber to feed the guards.

During the break, Louise Thuliez whispered to Edith, asking her opinion of the court proceedings so far.

"I think Baucq, Capiau, you, and I stand a bad chance," Edith whispered back. "But what does it matter so long as we are not shot?"

Edith had convinced herself from the time of her arrest that she would probably receive a sentence of two or three years in prison. As the trial proceeded, she held on to that belief. A penalty of death was beyond her imagining.

—

In the afternoon, the most heartbreaking scene of the trial took place when Stoeber called Philippe Bodart, the teenage son of Ada, to the witness stand. Philippe had spent the weeks since his arrest in prison. In court, Stoeber warned the boy that if he didn't tell the truth, he would be sent to prison for ten years of hard labor. Philippe was terrified, and he answered all the questions Stoeber asked about his mother's contribution to the secret organization. Philippe felt he had no choice. At the end of his testimony, he walked across the Senate chamber and hugged his mother.

—

Next morning, back in court, Stoeber made a speech for three and a half hours to the five judges. He outlined his case against the thirty-five defendants and asked the judges to find all thirty-five guilty of high treason. Each defendant, Stoeber argued, put the German army in extreme danger, and each deserved a sentence of severe punishment. Stoeber asked for the death penalty against nine of the defendants. One of the nine was Edith.

In the afternoon, the judges gave the lawyers for the defendants a chance to present a brief argument on behalf of their clients. For Edith, Sadi Kirschen returned to the point that her work with the escaping soldiers ended as soon as they crossed the border into Holland. Edith had no influence on what they did afterwards. If they returned to the fight against Germany, it was the soldiers' choice, not hers.

After the lawyers spoke, each defendant was permitted to make a short statement to the court. Edith's was the shortest of all, just a single sentence. "I have nothing to add," she said. Edith had decided that argument wouldn't have the slightest influence on the judges. Perhaps Stoeber's demand for the death sentence ended her hope. But if Edith wouldn't speak in her own defense, Princess Marie de Croy would. She told the judges to spare Edith. "If anyone should be punished," the princess said, when her turn came to address the tribunal, "it should be us and not her."

—

When Edith and the others left the courtroom on Friday afternoon, the court hadn't arrived at its verdict. The defendants were told the decision would come sometime later. It would be brought to them in the prison.

Friday night and all day Saturday went by without word from the court. The wait tortured the thirty-five defendants. What could they expect of the future? *Years in prison? Or even the death penalty?* During the hours in her cell, Edith read passages from her Bible and *The Imitation of Christ*. Philippe Baucq composed a sonnet to his wife. Albert Libiez wrote a story for his two children. The three of them felt as calm as they could under the circumstances.

A fellow defendant named Maurice Pansaers didn't have such a strong grip on his emotions. He was the owner of a coffee shop in Brussels who had sheltered English and French soldiers. On Saturday night in the prison, he gave in to despair, thinking he would never see freedom again. Pansaers hanged himself in his cell.

Sunday came and went, and finally, on Monday afternoon a little after four o'clock, prison guards led the thirty-four remaining defendants to the building's central hall. The prosecutor, Eduard Stoeber, was waiting for them, holding the court's verdict in his hands. Surrounded by soldiers and joined by the prison's German governor and a German priest, he read the verdict to the defendants.

The court acquitted nine of them. One was poor Maurice Pansaers. The miner Désiré Richez was another of the acquitted. Convictions were registered by the court against all of the rest. Most received prison sentences. Fifteen years at hard labor for Ada Bodart. The same for Herman Capiau and Albert Libiez. Ten years for the Princess de Croy.

Five of the defendants were sentenced to the firing squad. Stoeber read their names. Philippe Baucq. Louise Thuliez. Louis Séverin. Countess Jeanne de Belleville. And Edith Cavell.

As Edith's name was read, her face flushed as if she were about to faint. But the moment of weakness passed. Another of the defendants approached her and begged Edith to appeal to the Germans for mercy. The defendants had been told that an appeal was possible.

"It is useless," she said. "I am English, and they want my life."

Edith was right. A great hatred of England swept through Germany at the time. The Germans regarded the British as their most formidable enemy, and they expressed extreme dislike for everything and everyone connected to Britain. It would be a triumph to put to death the English Nurse Cavell.

Edith knew she was to be executed by a firing squad. What she didn't know was when. A German Lutheran pastor named Paul le Seur came to her later on Monday afternoon to tell her the day and time. The Germans had appointed le Seur to minister to all the prisoners. As le Seur entered Edith's cell, before he could get out a word, Edith asked him a direct question.

"How long will they give me?"

"Unfortunately," le Seur said, "only until the morning."

The Germans couldn't wait to execute Edith. Le Seur was saddened that his countrymen intended to put to death the woman who stood before him. He offered to be with Edith the following morning at the execution ground. Le Seur said he had never had the terrible experience of attending a death by firing squad, but he would stand by Edith at the end. Edith accepted le Seur's offer, and he left the cell.

—

At 8:30 that night, another clergyman came to Edith's cell. He was the Reverend Stirling Gahan, an Irishman and the only Anglican minister permitted by the Germans to carry on his ministry in Brussels during the war. He and his wife were Edith's friends. Gahan, a pious and amiable man, went to the Christmas party at the clinic when the English soldiers were in the basement. He knew about Edith's secret organization, but he took no part in it. He was too cautious for that.

His visit to Edith the night before her execution became important to her later place in history. It was to Gahan alone that she explained what she had learned from serving her country in the way she had. Gahan made no notes during his short time with Edith, and only the two of them were in the cell. But Gahan didn't doubt his accuracy when he later quoted Edith's words about heroism and patriotism from memory. The words that were later to become famous.

Edith was in her dressing gown when a guard showed Stirling Gahan into the cell. Always the perfect hostess, even on the night before her execution, Edith shook Gahan's hand and thanked him for coming. The clergyman's purpose in visiting Edith was to give her the Anglican Communion, something only an Anglican minister could perform. But first the two talked, Edith sitting on her bed and Gahan on the cell's only chair.

Edith told Gahan that she was thankful for the ten weeks in prison. It had been a rest from what she called "all earthly distractions and diversions." Then Edith spoke the lines about her ideas on patriotism that have been repeated in dozens of Cavell biographies and in thousands of newspaper and magazine articles about her life.

"This I would say," Edith told Gahan, "standing as I do in view of God and eternity, I realize that patriotism is not enough. I must have no hatred or bitterness for anyone."

The words must have seemed astonishingly generous, spoken by a woman who was to die in a few hours.

"We shall always remember you as a heroine and a martyr," Gahan said to Edith.

"Don't think of me like that," Edith replied, again surprising Gahan. "Think of me only as a nurse who tried to do her duty."

Gahan conducted the Communion ceremony, and together he and Edith repeated the words of the hymn "Abide with Me." Then Gahan said it was time to let Edith get some rest.

"Yes," she said, "I must be up at 5:00 AM."

—

It seems certain that the officials at St. Gilles told Edith that another of
the five defendants sentenced to death was to join her in the execution
next morning. Philippe Baucq would be shot at the same time as Edith.

In their cells that last night, Baucq and Edith wrote love letters.
Baucq's was to his wife. Edith's was to her nurses at the clinic. She told
the young women that they might have felt she was unjustly hard on them
at times during their training, but the truth was that she had loved them
much more than they knew. She warned the nurses against the danger of
causing unhappiness to others through a careless word. "Never speak
evil," Edith instructed them.

—

In the early morning of October 12, Elisabeth Wilkins and another
English nurse from the clinic, Beatrice Smith, stood outside St. Gilles
Prison in the rain that was falling on Brussels. Both knew about the execution, and they had been waiting for almost two hours to say a silent
good-bye to their Matron. At five o'clock, they watched as two German
military cars drove out of the prison. Edith, wearing the same clothes
she wore at her trial and carrying her beloved book, *The Imitation of
Christ*, sat in the backseat of the first car. Two German soldiers were on
either side of her, and Pastor Paul le Seur rode in the front seat.
Philippe Baucq, two German soldiers, and a Catholic priest named
Leyendecker were in the second car. Wilkins felt sure that Edith realized the two nurses were in the street, though Edith neither waved nor
nodded in their direction. She was a woman who would never make the
slightest scene.

—

The place of execution was Belgium's national shooting range, the grounds
where soldiers practiced their accuracy with rifles and pistols. The range,

a sprawling building with a large open space at the rear, was in Schaerbeck, the Brussels suburb where Baucq had lived with his family.

When the two cars reached the range, German soldiers whisked Edith, Baucq, and the two clergymen down the corridors that led to the execution ground in the back. Just before the party reached its destination, Pastor le Seur offered Edith a bottle of smelling salts to calm her nerves. Edith said she had no need for smelling salts, but she asked le Seur to do her a final favor. Borrowing a pen, she wrote her name in *The Imitation of Christ*, followed by "With love to E.D. Cavell." She closed the book and asked le Seur to see that it reached her cousin Eddy. At the very end of her life, she was thinking of the cousin she might have married. Le Seur promised he would do as Edith asked, and he was as good as his word. (It's not certain when Eddy received the book, but after it came into his hands, he published *The Imitation of Christ* in what he called the Edith Cavell Edition. It included all of Edith's underlinings and notes, including her last inscription to Eddy.)

As Edith and Baucq arrived at the execution ground, a company of 250 German soldiers stood to attention. Several German officials silently received the two prisoners. Among the officials was Eduard Stoeber, the prosecutor who took a leading role in each fateful event in the last days of Edith's life.

Stoeber's final job was to read aloud the sentences of death to Edith and Baucq. The two of them stood in front of the company of soldiers, le Seur alongside Edith and Leyendecker with Baucq. But before Stoeber could begin, Baucq spoke out in loud clear French. "Comrades," he said to the 250 soldiers, "in death we are all comrades. . . ."

Baucq wanted to say more, but an officer warned him to be silent. Then Stoeber read the sentences in German and French. When he finished, le Seur stepped closer to Edith and softly recited a short prayer. Edith pressed his hand. She spoke for the last time.

"Ask Mr. Gahan," she said to le Seur, "to tell my loved ones later on that my soul, as I believe, is safe and that I am glad to die for my country."

Le Seur led Edith a few steps to a pole. He waited while a soldier tied her loosely to the pole and blindfolded her eyes. At the same time, Baucq was escorted to a second pole by the Catholic priest, Leyendecker. The two poles stood several meters apart. Facing the poles, six paces away, were two firing squads of eight soldiers each.

Le Seur moved away from Edith. He expected that the command to shoot would come immediately. But a delay followed, one that le Seur later wrote felt like an eternity. At Baucq's pole, Leyendecker and Baucq were still speaking. Baucq, who refused to wear a blindfold, had a few final words to get off his chest. He refused to rush his own execution. Edith stood waiting, patient and enduring to the end.

Leyendecker walked away from Baucq at last, and an officer called the command to shoot. The sound of sixteen firing rifles crashed through the stillness of the early morning. Edith dropped forward from her pole. One shot had hit her in the middle of the forehead; other shots caught her in the heart. No one at the scene doubted that she died instantly.

Two graves had already been dug at the execution ground. Edith's body was placed in a plain wooden coffin and lowered into one grave, Baucq's coffin into the other. Both graves were marked with simple wooden crosses, carrying only their names. PHILIPPE BAUCQ appeared on one cross. EDITH CAVELL was painted on the other. The Germans, so anxious to be rid of Edith, buried her in the most anonymous graveyard in all of Brussels.

OPPOSITE: *After Edith's execution, the Germans buried her in this humble cemetery on the shooting range just steps from the spot where the firing squad shot her.* (The Royal London Hospital Archives)

"SHE DIED LIKE A HEROINE."

Chapter Twelve

EDITH'S LEGACY

O n October 21, a few days after word of Edith's execution blazed across the front pages of Britain's newspapers, the bishop of London preached about her in a special ceremony at the church of St. Martin-in-the-Fields. He said that Britain didn't need a campaign to recruit more soldiers; Edith's execution was incentive all by itself for young men to join the armed forces. The bishop was right. In the two months preceding Edith's death, the enlistment rate into the British Expeditionary Force averaged just under five thousand men per week. In the two months following news of her execution reaching Britain, the weekly average jumped to over ten thousand.

Britain issued thousands of posters and postcards after Edith's execution. The pictures, intended as propaganda to stir citizens against the Germans, weren't always accurate. This idealized poster shows Edith in her uniform, which she didn't wear on the day she died, nor does the poster reveal Edith's fatal bullet wounds to her forehead and chest. (The Royal London Hospital Archives)

The same thing happened in France and in the countries of the British Empire. Fired up by Edith's courageous example, and furious at the barbarian Germans, young men rushed to enlistment offices. Edith had inspired them to go to war. Britain's politicians seized on Edith as a propaganda tool, playing up the need to follow her path. "She has taught the bravest men among us the supreme lesson of courage," Britain's Prime Minister Herbert Asquith said in the House of Commons. But his words were hardly needed. The story of Edith Cavell had already taken hold on the public's imagination, and fighting men marched to war in her memory.

—

In Brussels, in the days after Edith's execution, three other members of the secret network – Louise Thuliez, Countess Jeanne de Belleville, and Louis Séverin – waited at St. Gilles Prison to take their turn before the firing squad. But for them, death never came. The Germans were stunned at the worldwide revulsion stirred by Edith's execution. Germany's leader, Kaiser Wilhelm II, announced that, from then on, no woman would be shot unless he consented. He gave the impression that consent would never come from him. The kaiser's announcement was too late to repair the damage that Germany had done to its reputation. But the lives of the three prisoners in St. Gilles were saved. The Germans converted the death sentences of Thuliez, de Belleville, and Séverin to terms in prison.

These three and their colleagues in the secret organization didn't go free until the end of the war. All survived their imprisonment, though Ada Bodart never recovered from the experience and died not long after, ill and penniless (the fate of Bodart's teenage son, Philippe, was never known). Princess de Croy returned to her château at Bellignies, and Louise Thuliez went back to teaching school. Everybody reclaimed their old lives. Albert Libiez, the Mons lawyer, took up his practice, and years later, in the Second World War, he once again worked secretly against Germany.

This time, when he was caught, the German Nazis sent him to a concentration camp where Libiez died, leaving behind a record as a fighter of injustice in two world wars.

—

In November 1915, Nurse Elisabeth Wilkins decided Brussels was too dangerous for her. The Germans had been rounding up evidence against Wilkins, and she thought her days of freedom might soon be over. When she fled back to Britain, she took Grace Jemmett with her. Jemmett went to live with her parents, while Wilkins continued her career in nursing, ending it as Matron at a hospital in Somerset County.

Jackie, the dog, left Brussels too. After his mistress' execution, he was sent to Bellignies, where he lived until his death in 1923. Princess de Croy, his last mistress, arranged for him to be embalmed. Then she shipped Jackie's stuffed body to Norwich, where, odd as it seems, it was put on display for decades as the faithful pet of Britain's heroine.

—

The war lasted until November 11, 1918. From mid-1915 to late 1918, the fighting raged on several fronts: in Russia to the east; in Turkey, where the Turks fought as Germany's ally; and at sea, where the Germans battled Britain's traditionally powerful navy. But the most decisive warfare took place on the western front in northeastern France and in parts of Belgium. It was in the trenches of the west that the armies fought the war to its conclusion.

The battle wasn't continuous, but more a long and terrible standoff interrupted by individual clashes. These were bloody and futile. Both sides, Germany and the Allied nations, faced one another along a front of 465 miles, from the border of one neutral country, Switzerland, to the border of another neutral country, Holland. Ten thousand Allied soldiers were packed into each mile of the front lines, with thousands more ready to move up. When they went into periodic battle, the results were grim.

On a single summer day in 1916, in one episode at the Battle of the Somme in France, fifty thousand British troops died as they advanced straight into German fire. The deaths produced no strategic result, not moving the Allied front at the Somme from the spot it had been in at the beginning of the day. In the last three years of the war, 3 million men from the Allied armies died along the length of the western trenches. Throughout the slaughter, the front stayed essentially in place, the Allies pushing ahead not much more than five miles in the entire three years.

The Americans joined the war on the Allies' side in 1917, drawn into the conflict by two German blunders. The first came when Germany killed 128 American citizens in the sinking of the passenger liner *Lusitania* in 1915. The other involved German agents that set out to provoke a diversionary war in America's neighbor Mexico. Those events, plus America's lingering horror at Edith Cavell's execution, stirred the United States to combat. The country's entry into the war and the British invention of the tank combined to give the Allies an edge over the Germans.

But fatigue decided the war in the end. Over the years of fighting, both sides wore down. Millions of men died, and millions more suffered wounds. The soldiers grew sick of the massacre, which came to seem pointless. Everyone was tired, but the Germans tired first. As several historians later wrote, it could just as easily have been one of the Allies, perhaps France or Russia, who decided to quit the fighting before anyone else. But Germany was the country that surrendered on November 11, 1918, and the killing finally stopped.

—

On March 17, 1919, in a ceremony in Brussels, an official British party, which included the king and queen of England, removed Edith's body from the grave on the shooting range. The exhumation was the first step in her

At a ceremony in March 1919, Edith's body was removed from its original grave in Brussels for reburial on the grounds of Norwich Cathedral in England. Attending the ceremony were King George V and Queen Mary of England and, in the rear wearing all the medals, King Albert I of Belgium. (The Royal London Hospital Archives)

reburial at home in Norfolk. The trip from Brussels to Norwich proceeded in stages, lasting three days altogether, with several stops for ceremonies recognizing Edith's courage and sacrifice. Accompanying the coffin were Edith's two sisters, Florence and Lillian. Edith's mother had died less than a year earlier, distraught and bewildered by her oldest daughter's execution.

When the cortège traveled by train from Dover to London, church bells rang in every village and people lined the tracks, their heads bowed. In London, the first half of the burial service took place at Westminster Abbey, then the mourners got back on the train to Norwich for the rest of the service. Edith's brother, Jack, joined the crowd at Norwich's famous cathedral. So did the man who could have become Edith's husband, Eddy Cavell. At the service, Bishop Bertram Pollock of Norwich remembered Edith in her youth. He said she was "an innocent, unselfish, devout and pretty girl."

Edith was reburied in a plot at the rear of the cathedral. Her final resting place was small and inconspicuous, marked by a plain white stone cross. Even the simple grave might have been too showy for the modest Edith.

—

Edith would have felt just as embarrassed by the number of ways that England and other countries continued to pay tribute to her. Renowned English actresses played Edith in the story of her life on the screen and on the stage: Sybil Thorndike in a 1928 movie, Anna Neagle in a 1939 film, and Joan Plowright in a 1982 play. Around the world, everything from streets to mountains were named after Edith. In the town of Beaulieu-sur-Mer, on France's Mediterranean, a pretty road was renamed Rue Edith Cavell in gratitude for all the French soldiers rescued by Edith. And Canada put her name on a peak in the Rocky Mountains near Jasper, Alberta. The peak, 3,363 meters high, became Mount Edith Cavell.

OPPOSITE, CLOCKWISE FROM TOP LEFT:

This stone memorial stands outside the Institut Edith Cavell in Brussels. It celebrates both Edith and Marie Depage, wife of Dr. Antoine Depage who founded the clinic that later became the Institut. (The Royal London Hospital Archives)

The memorial to Edith in front of Norwich Cathedral describes her as "nurse, patriot and martyr." She took great pride in her career as a nurse, but she never thought of herself as a martyr. (Jack Batten)

Communities all over the world honored Edith by putting her name on streets and avenues. This sign borders a road running through the pretty little town of Beaulieu-sur-Mer on the French Riviera. (Marjorie Harris)

This sign in the East End of Toronto faces a street originally named Dresden Avenue. Toronto's city council changed the name in the spring of 1916 as a gesture to honor Edith. (Jack Batten)

In England, Belgium, and countless other countries, governments and citizens made sure that Edith's name would never fade from memory. A new nurses' residence, built at the London Hospital in 1916, was intended to be named Alexandra Home, after the widow of King Edward VII, but with Queen Alexandra's approval, the name was changed to Edith Cavell Home. In Brussels, the clinic where Edith served as the first Matron came to be called the Cavell Institute. A bust of her stands outside Norwich Cathedral, and a large bas-relief showing Edith and two soldiers, put up by the Societa Italo-Canadese on November 11, 1922, occupies a plaza in front of the Toronto General Hospital.

—

The best-known Cavell memorial is the statue of Edith that faces south across Trafalgar Square in London. The statue shows Edith looking far more imposing than she ever was in life. Below the statue, the pedestal carries Edith's name, together with the place, date, and time of her execution. That was all the information on the pedestal when the memorial was unveiled in the early 1920s. But in 1924, a man named F.W. Jowitt, the commissioner of public works in the government of the day, decided that the pedestal needed more. He ordered that Edith's declaration to the Reverend Stirling Gahan on the last night of her life be carved into the stone under the date of her death:

PATRIOTISM IS NOT ENOUGH. I MUST HAVE NO HATRED OR BITTERNESS FOR ANYONE.

The words were Edith's message to the world. She helped hundreds of her fellow countrymen escape the German enemy, an action that showed how much her country meant to her. But simple patriotism didn't go far enough. It couldn't prevent wars; it might even encourage them. In Edith's opinion, the only course of action was to reach out and accept all men and women, no matter what countries they came from. In saying her two famous lines, Edith was only doing her duty as she saw it.

SELECTED BIBLIOGRAPHY

Clark-Kennedy, A.E. *Edith Cavell, Pioneer and Patriot*. Faber. 1965.

Daunton, Claire. *Edith Cavell: Her Life and Her Art*. Royal London Hospital. 1990.

Elkon, Juliette. *Edith Cavell*. Messner. 1956.

Felstead, Theodore. *Edith Cavell. The Crime That Shocked the World*. Newman. 1940.

Gill, Gillian. *Nightingales: The Extraordinary Upbringing and Curious Life of Miss Florence Nightingale*. Ballantine. 2004.

Gorrell, Gena K. *Heart and Soul: The Story of Florence Nightingale*. Tundra Books. 2000.

Keegan, John. *The First World War*. Random House. 2000.

Peachment, Brian. *Ready to Die: The Story of Edith Cavell*. Pergamon Press. 1980.

Ryder, Rowland. *Edith Cavell*. Hamish Hamilton. 1975.

Strachan, Hew. *The First World War*. Viking. 2004.

Strachey, Lytton. *Eminent Victorians*. Bloomsbury. 1918.

ACKNOWLEDGMENTS

The following people and institutions were exceptionally generous in providing research materials, illustrations, and support. Sarah Batten. Rebecca Snow. Chris Harris. Peter Smith. Janet Inkstetter. The Royal London Hospital Archives and Museum, particularly Jonathan Evans, Kate Richardson, and Sarah Coombs. The Imperial War Museum. The church of St. Mary the Virgin in Swardeston, Norfolk, particularly Churchwarden Nick Miller. The Reference Library of the Toronto Public Library. Tundra Books, particularly Sue Tate and Kathy Lowinger. And, as ever, Marjorie Harris.

INDEX